Of all the halls of heaven, the hall of music is
the lowest and the smallest, but he who wants
to approach God, has only to enter this hall.

Rabbi Uri of Strelisk, *The Seraph*

VELVEL PASTERNAK

Beyond Hava Nagila

Hasidic Music in 3 Movements

tara publications

HASIDIC MUSIC COLLECTIONS
By Velvel PASTERNAK

Chabad Melodies
Hasidic Hits
Hasidic Israeli Club Date
Modzitzer Melodies
Rejoice-Songs in Modern Hasidic Style
Songs of Joy
Songs of the Hasidim Vols. 1 & 2
The Best of Hasidic Song
The Best of the Hasidic Song Festivals
The Shlomo Carlebach Anthology
The Simcha Songbook
Ura-Hasidic Style Songs

ISBN 0-933676-78-6

Printed in the United States of America

CONTENTS

FOREWORD

Most books written about Jewish music are directed primarily at the musician or the student of music. Interested lay people, even those with some musical knowledge, often find such books difficult to get into and even more difficult to get through. In this volume, I have tried to minimize technical aspects in favor of annotations and personal reminiscences in order to make hasidic music interesting and understandable to the broad-based public. At the same time, the professional musician and student should find information that is not readily available elsewhere.

The format of this book has been designed with the lay person in mind. I am hopeful that the folksier nature of the opening section will entice people to read further and discover this true folk music heritage. To make the music examples more relevant for those who may have difficulty with music in transcription, a 70-minute compact disc containing previously recorded hasidic music is enclosed.

ACKNOWLEDGMENTS

I am grateful and indebted to the following: my sister, Sarah Halberstam, for her careful reading of the text and most valuable suggestions; Barbara Cinnamon, a good friend, for concrete and constructive editorial advice; above all, my daughter, Shira Be'eri, for meticulous and painstaking editing. Her insightful and creative additions have added immeasurably to the style and flow of the textual portions of this book; my son, Mayer, whose devotion to Tara Publications has afforded me the freedom to engage in areas of development, research and writing; Goldie, my partner in life, who, as always, ungrudgingly and graciously afforded me the "space" to research in the vineyard of Jewish music and bring an additional manuscript to completion.

V. P.

LIST OF MUSIC EXAMPLES

Page no.

CD-Selections

1. **RIKUD-MODZITZ**
Recording: *Music of Modzitz*
2. **KI ONU AMECHO**
Recording: *Songs of the Lubavitcher Chasidim*
3. **EN KITZVO**
Recording: *Modzitzer Favorites*
4. **WALTZ**
Recording: *Modzitzer Favorites*
5. **ESO ENAI**
Recording: *Hanshomo Loch*
6. **ALTER REBBE'S NIGUN**
Recording: *The Klezmer Violin*
7. **ELI ATA**
Recording: The World's Most Beautiful Jewish Songs
8. **A DUDELE**
Recording: Jan Peerce-The Final Recording
9. **ETZ CHAYIM HI**
Recording: *Tanchumim*
10. **MAZURKA**
Recording: *Modzitzer Favorites II*
11. **BRIDER, BRIDER**
Recording: *Songs of the Bobover Chasidim*
12. **NYE ZURITSE CHLOPTSI**
Recording: *Songs of the Lubavitcher Chasidim*
13. **MISERLOU**
14. **NAPOLEON'S MARCH**
Recording: *Chabad Nigunim Vol. II*
15. **MI HO'ISH**
Recording: *The Rabbis' Sons*
16. **FIRST "OPERA"**
Recording: *Music of Modzitz*

Andante

Reminiscence, Research & Recordings

TO THE STRAINS OF A MELODY

Among the many legends that highlight the unique position of song in hasidic life, is the story concerning Rabbi Moshe Leib of Sassov, known throughout Eastern Europe as the Sassover Rebbe. The Sassover Rebbe took upon himself the duty of assisting poor brides financially and providing them with the basic necessities for married life. When he was able to accomplish this, his final act was attending their weddings. One day, at the nuptial ceremony of an orphaned bride, the itinerant *klezmer* musicians played a melody which impressed the Rebbe. He was overheard saying that it was his wish that this same tune would accompany his burial. Many years later the Rebbe died, and hundreds of hasidim traveled from many parts of Europe to accompany him to the cemetery and eternal rest. At a crossroads the mourners suddenly saw a group of musicians sitting in a horse-drawn cart. The hasidim assumed that these musicians were on their way to a wedding. With unexpected suddenness, the horse broke into a gallop and whisked the musicians away. When the funeral procession arrived at the cemetery entrance, the hasidim were greeted by these same musicians, who now had their instruments in playing position. The hasidim were angered and could only assume that the musicians had come to mock the proceedings. What other reason could musicians have for being at a funeral? Suddenly, one of the older hasidim remembered the Rebbe's wish of long ago, that a specific tune be played at his burial. Consternation broke out within the group. Until the time of the Second Temple in Jerusalem, a husband was obligated to hire two wind instrumentalists to accompany the casket of his departed wife. After the destruction of the Temple, however, it was decreed that musical instruments should not be used. Two thousand years of tradition proclaimed that music should not be played at a funeral. Yet, an eyewitness heard the Rebbe declare his wish for a melody to accompany his burial. "What should be done?"

In traditional Jewish life, legal questions are solved by a *bet din* (a religious court of law). A rabbinical court was hastily formed from among the learned hasidim, and piles of rocks were assembled in order that the judges could sit during their deliberation. The verdict, which broke with long-standing tradition, was that the wish of the Sassover Rebbe must be honored. The witness, an old man, was asked if he could recall the melody. After answering in the affirmative, he approached the musicians and hummed a few bars. Then the musicians took up the strains of the melody. As the Rebbe's body was lowered into the ground, it was accompanied by a melody which many years before had brought a poor orphaned bride to the *chupah* (wedding canopy).

Of all the stories related to hasidic music, no other story has quite the force and emotional appeal for a musician as this one. Longstanding tradition is broken, and music becomes, not only the accompanying motif of one's life, but also the companion of the hasid on his eternal journey. The soul, in returning to the Maker, ascends to the strains of a melody.

"One *nigun* can express more than a thousand words."

—Tsadik of Kuzmir

SINCE MY FATHER'S *Z'MIROT*

My love for hasidic music goes back to my childhood in Toronto, Canada, when my father sang *zmirot* at the *Shabbos* table. My father did not have a beautiful voice, but he was compensated musically with a remarkable ear. In my father's hometown in Poland, he had become especially fond of the *nigunim* composed by the Rebbes of Modzitz. He could remember and sing a Modzitzer *nigun* perfectly after hearing it only a few times. Individuals in the Toronto Jewish community invariably turned to him for the correct version of a Modzitzer *nigun*.

During my youth, a piano was considered *treif* (not kosher). It was not that Orthodox Jews found anything inherently bad in this instrument, but the unspoken fear existed that proficiency in playing might lead to a concert career. Since most music events took place Friday night or Saturday, desecration of the Jewish Sabbath by playing a musical instrument was almost a foregone conclusion. It was much easier to do away with such potential problems by keeping the piano out of an Orthodox Jewish home.

In the 1940s, the educational system instituted in the Toronto public schools was emulated throughout Canada. In addition to the very strong attention given the three R's, regular short periods of music study were given to all grade school students. I found *solfeggio* (music reading) intriguing, and I was able to transfer the *do re mi's* I learned to the piano whenever I could find one. When I was twelve, my mother, having concluded that a piano was not *treif* after all, bought a used one and engaged a teacher for my six year old sister and myself. The teacher, a pleasant lady, was quite conservative in her approach to students and piano study. Although I was able to "play by ear" with two hands, she nevertheless insisted that I begin at the most elementary level. I tried very hard to do the finger-play and scales assigned, but after each lesson, I was again playing in my own fashion, turning the dozens of folksongs I had learned in school into easy, self-taught piano settings. After several months of lessons, I begged my mother to give lessons only to my sister, and I continued to play by ear.

While still in high school, I became the music counselor in a Zionist co-ed summer camp on the outskirts of Toronto. My only qualification for the job was piano playing. I taught the campers songs by rote and worked in conjunction with the dramatic counselor on various musical productions. Although Toronto became one of the premier Jewish communities in the last quarter of the twentieth century, it was quite difficult to receive an intensive post-elementary school Jewish education during the early 1950s. Accordingly, each year a number of boys between the ages of fourteen and eighteen were enrolled in New York yeshivas to continue their high school and college education. Yeshiva University, the institution I chose, offered the opportunity to study Judaic and secular studies under one roof. My family and friends assumed that I would study for the rabbinate, and would take a synagogue pulpit after graduating. Music, however, kept gnawing at me and I was fortunate to find a music teacher and mentor, although under strange circumstances.

A number of Yeshiva University students served as waiters and busboys in a Catskill Mountains resort during Passover. While walking in town one day, several of these young men saw a customer being evicted from a bar. Why they stopped to engage the "drunk" in conversation I never did find out. I did discover that this so-called drunk, Dr. Charles Gay, held doctoral degrees in music and psychology. Intrigued by his intelligent conversation, the yeshiva students promised to be in contact with him in New York after the holiday. They kept their promise, and one of them suggested that he become a vocal coach for professional cantors. It did not matter that Gay was not Jewish, and within six months, by recommendation only, he was coaching more than a dozen professional and would be cantors.

A twenty-one-year-old with only a little musical knowledge remembered from grade school, I turned to Gay and asked him if he could make me proficient in music theory. Because I was interested in this aspect rather than in vocal training, he accepted me as a new student, but on condition. He would take no payment for the lessons. In exchange, I would keep him company in his local bar after each lesson. For more than a year I frequented the bar, conversed with him on a wide range of topics and watched him drink rye whiskey followed by a glass of milk. He told me that the milk provided a lining for his ulcerated stomach. When I was with him in the bar on Friday afternoon, Gay would often look at his watch. He knew Sabbath candle lighting time on any given Friday, and would make sure that I left the bar with enough time to return to my dorm before the beginning of Sabbath.

When he felt that I was ready, I took a qualifying exam and entered the Extension Division of the Juilliard School of Music where, among other things, I took courses in choral conducting and Literature and Materials of Music. At the end of the academic year, faculty members from Columbia University were invited to speak to the Juilliard students. They made us aware that performing careers were limited, and those needing to earn a living, at least in the short term, would do well to study for a Masters degree in music education. I took the suggestion and, along with a number of other Juilliard students, I enrolled in Columbia. I received a Masters degree the following year and an unexpected bonus. Goldie Garber, a young lady who specialized in early childhood education, was my fellow student in a course, Music for Children. Our relationship blossomed, and, several months after receiving my graduate degree, we were married.

Personnel at the Board of Jewish Education in New York City encouraged me to look for work in the Jewish education sector rather than in the public school system. Harry Coopersmith, the music consultant for the Board at the time, sent me to interview for a position at the Brandeis School in Woodmere, Long Island. Brandeis, one of the first Jewish day schools in the United States, was known for its quality secular education as well as Judaic studies. I called and set up an appointment with the headmistress, Helen Feinberg. As I introduced myself to her secretary, I was informed that she was temporarily busy in one of the classrooms. I was told that she would be back shortly and that I should make myself comfortable in her office. I sat down, took out my diplomas and other pertinent documents and waited for her. She greeted me as she came into the room and, out of the corner of her eye, noticed a diploma. She looked at it incredulously and said.

"Young man is that really your name?

"Yes," I responded.

" Velvel, oh that's awful!" she said.

"But this is the name I have always had."

"I'm sorry," she said.

"But that is the name my mother gave me at birth. It was my grandfather Velvel's name."

"Young man," she said, "before we can offer you employment in this school, you will have to promise to change your name.

Slightly agitated, I asked for the reason and it was quick in coming. In 1957, a talented ventriloquist named Ricky Lane, often appeared with his dummy, Velvel, on one of the major TV networks. The headmistress thought that it could be quite traumatic for her students to have a teacher named Velvel when a dummy with the same name appeared on television. Although it would be quite difficult to think of myself as anything but Velvel, I realized that I was to be married shortly and needed the security of knowing that rent money was in place. I therefore promised Mrs. Feinberg that if I took the job, I would change Velvel to William.

I took the position and, for the next five years, I was known as William within the confines of the school. Outside the Brandeis School I was still known as Velvel. I had been in the school for only two weeks when the door to the music room opened one day and an individual with a goatee and a broad smile said, "Velvel Pasternak, *shalom alechem*." I returned the greeting. He introduced himself as Rabbi

Binyamin Kamenetsky and said that he remembered me as a child in Toronto. His father, Rabbi Yaakov Kamenetsky, a world-renowned rabbinic authority, served the Toronto Jewish community for many years as one of its leading rabbis. We spoke for a while and he informed me that he had just opened a yeshiva with separate divisions for both boys and girls in a building three blocks from the Brandeis School. He had come to offer me a *mitzva*. The yeshiva students needed *ruach* that he felt I could supply through Jewish music. As far as he knew, the piano in the Yeshiva did not have eighty-eight working keys, nor did the school have money to pay me at the time. It was a week before Yom Kippur, a time when many Jews look for *mitzvos* to add to their personal account in the "Book of Life." Without searching for one, a *mitzva* was brought to me in the Brandeis classroom. I accepted.

Beginning in mid-October, after finishing at the Brandeis School in the afternoon, I gave music classes on two successive days to the boys and girls of the Yeshiva. One afternoon in November, while on my way to the Yeshiva of South Shore, I heard the name William from across the street. Because I did not think of myself as William outside the Brandeis School building, I did not think of responding. When it persisted, I looked up and saw Mrs. Feinberg on the other side of the street. She motioned that I should cross over.

"William," she said, "from my window I have noticed you jogging several times after school. Could I be inquisitive and ask you if you are doing this for health reasons"

"Oh no," I said, "I am just going over to the Yeshiva of South Shore on Oak Street."

Her face turned a little pale and she asked, "What do you do there?"

"Oh, it is a poor struggling school and the rabbi asked me to give music sessions to his students."

She put her hand on my shoulder and in a barely audible whisper said,

"William, you must not teach there."

"Why not?" I said, slightly annoyed.

"Well, I passed by the school several weeks ago and the windows were open, and I saw all those boys. You know, William, they all shake."

"Of course they shake, "I said.

"But why, William, why? It looks diseased."

Well, there I was on a street in the prestigious Five Towns of Long Island trying to convince my headmistress that *shokling* (bodily shaking while praying) was not due to an aberration of the spinal column nor was it any way indicative of St. Vitas Dance.

"But why do they shake?" She asked again.

"I really don't know," I replied. "Probably because their parents and their grandparents before them also shook. It is a physical reaction of the body to the act of praying. "

She had difficulty accepting my explanation and I truly believe that she never fully forgave me for teaching in the Yeshiva of South Shore. Because the Brandeis School was recognized throughout Long Island as a model, progressive school, visitors from Long Island educational institutions and student teachers would often come to observe its various programs. At the end of these visits, the Brandeis staff would be formally introduced. Mrs. Feinberg always saved my introduction for last and her words were invariably the same:

"And this is our music director, William Pasternak, who, in addition to his duties in our school, is also the music teacher at the *Shaker School* on Oak Street."

I was, however, grateful to Mrs. Feinberg and the Brandeis School for affording me the opportunity to edit and arrange music for six recordings of hasidic music during the early 1960s. The Brandeis teaching schedule was such that no specialty teacher worked more than an hour and a half without a half hour to forty-five minute break following. Thus, on any given day I did not work more than four hours. When I began to teach, I would read novels between classes. Later, I found a fold up cot and stretched out for a short nap the minute my students left. Soon this seemed to be a waste of precious time. When the opportunity to do recordings came along, I used every minute of the break times to prepare, edit and arrange music. My recordings of the Modzitzer and Bobover hasidim were arranged in Brandeis. I continued arranging and recording hasidic music through 1966.

In early 1967, I received a rather frantic call from the mother of a bride in Sheboygan, Wisconsin. She informed me that her daughter was to be married in a few months and that her future son-in-law, who lived in New York, was planning to bring a number of his yeshiva classmates as guests. Not having access to a band that could play traditional Jewish music in Sheboygan, she scouted nearby Chicago, the city with the largest Jewish population in the mid-west, in the hopes of finding a suitable instrumental ensemble. When she asked various bandleaders if they knew Jewish music, she was informed that they could play *Hava Nagila* and *Dayenu*. "Mr. Pasternak," she said, "can these young men dance all night to only two songs? Please speak to my daughter and help us. You will be doing a great *mitzvah* (good deed). Since my family and yeshiva education had made me aware of the importance of performing *mitzvos*, I said, "I'll be happy to talk to her."

The soon-to-be bride repeated the problem and offered to purchase a book of traditional Jewish melodies. I could almost feel the depth of her dejection through the telephone headset when I informed her that no such collection existed. "How much will you charge to write out music for me?" she asked. I told her that if she would send me a listing of the songs needed, I would transcribe them and she could pay me only for my time spent. Her list of fifteen songs arrived several days later and I began transcribing the melodies in pencil, adding guitar chords for accompaniment. I mailed the sheet music to the young lady and informed her that I had spent two and a half hours on the transcriptions. Payment of $25.00 (quite adequate remuneration for that period of time) and a thank you note arrived very quickly. It was not until the wedding had passed that I received a letter from the bride and her family with profuse thanks for enabling them and the Jewish community of Sheboygan to witness and participate in a "wonderful, traditional *simcha*." I felt truly rewarded.

Several months later, I received a call from a woman in Florida. She introduced herself and said, "We were at a wedding in Sheboygan and we have the same problem in Florida." For a moment I could not recall the wedding to which she referred or the nature of her similar problem. She told me that her daughter was getting married and needed traditional Jewish music for the bandleader in her area. I realized that I had sent the originals to Sheboygan, and getting them back from the Chicago bandleader could prove to be problematic as well as time consuming. I wrote out the melodies again, this time photocopying the music sheets and keeping the originals. Remuneration and a thank you note for helping to make a "wonderful *simcha* in Florida" came quickly. During the next six months, by word of mouth only, my music sheets of traditional and Hasidic melodies made their way to bandleaders in a number of cities including Boston, Los Angeles, Dallas and Toronto

Realizing that there seemed to be a need for sheet music of traditional Jewish songs, I began collecting material. Because I had arranged and conducted eleven recordings of hasidic music, including Modzitz, Ger, Bobov, and Lubavitch, I had enough material to get started. In the summer of 1967, I began editing and arranging most of these recorded melodies, and others for publication. In addition to transcribing the music, I transliterated, translated, annotated the song texts, and prepared an introduction and discography. The manuscript was ready in the summer of 1968, and I looked for a publisher of Jewish music. I found only one that seemed viable, Metro Music, located on Second Avenue, the home of the Yiddish Theater in New York City. The owner of Metro Music gave me a little under ten minutes of his time and said, "Young man I don't think that you will be able to sell ten copies of a hasidic music book." It was disconcerting, to say the least, to be told that more than a year's effort would result in almost no sales. Undaunted, I pressed on. When all the Jewish publishers that I approached, turned me down, I tried the general music publishers in the United States. The first of these publishers asked for a projection as to how many thousands of copies I felt could be sold during the first year of publication. I hid my chuckle and thought: a Jewish music publisher projected sales of less then ten copies while a general publisher spoke in terms of thousands.

When publishers did not seem to be the answer, "vanity press" (self-publishing) was suggested. Many charitable foundations in the United States, I was told, might help fund such a book. A Foundation Directory provided me with the names of seventy-four foundations who indicated an interest in preserving the heritage of East-European Jewish music. My formal requests to seventy-three foundations were unanswered. One of them returned my original letter with the words, "our funds are committed, good luck," hand written in the margin.

My stress and frustration resulted in a spastic colon and the need for weeks of medication. While on the mend, another avenue was suggested to me—individual Jewish philanthropists. The most promising seemed to be a gentleman who had helped establish collections of Jewish music in a number of libraries in the United States and Israel. After studying my proposal, his secretary called me. I can recall the conversation almost verbatim:

"Mr. Pasternak this is in response to your hasidic music book proposal. My employer is very interested in this. Tell me, does this collection have music of Lubavitch?"

I replied, "yes."

"And does it have music of Modzitz?"

Again, I replied, "yes."

"And Bobov?"

"Yes."

"And Vishnitz?"

"Yes"

"And Ger?"

"Yes."

"Wonderful," said the caller. "My employer would like three copies of the manuscript. He needs two for the Jewish music libraries in the United States and one for the library at the Hebrew University in Jerusalem."

"If your employer read my proposal, he must have seen that I am trying to put together funds to have the manuscript published," I said.

"My employer is not interested in the financial aspects. He is only interested in obtaining three copies of the manuscript."

"I am sorry, but I cannot give out copies of an unpublished manuscript," I said.

"Thank you," he replied, and the line was dead.

Several weeks later, during family dinner, I again received a phone call from the philanthropist's secretary.

"Good evening, Mr. Pasternak. My employer has a suggestion for you." For a moment, I felt excitement. Perhaps this was an offer of partial funding.

"If you will print the book in Israel, it will cost much cheaper. Thank you." And with that the conversation ended.

I shook my head in disbelief. I realized that any attempt at funding the book from outside sources was futile. It would have to be a vanity publication sponsored by my own funds. I was encouraged to send out a pre-publication offering to cantors and professional Jewish musicians who might be acquainted with my name and the recordings of hasidic music. I composed a letter.

" I am delighted to inform you that..."

By chance, before the letter was sent, I showed it to a friend who had experience in advertising.

"Do you know what most people do with letters that begin, 'I am delighted to inform you?'" he asked. "They are usually filed quickly—most often in a garbage can." I imposed on him to offer a better opening sentence and he suggested, "Have you ever heard a hasidic melody and hoped that someone would write it down? Well, we have done just that!"

I retyped the letter and shortly thereafter it was sent to one thousand cantors, rabbis, Jewish music educators and musicians. The pre-publication offering price for the projected 170 page hardbound edition, *Songs of the Hasidim*, was $7.50, including shipping. Within four weeks, I received pre-paid orders from more than 300 individuals. For each order received, I sent a return post card with my gratitude and promise that the completed book would be sent out within two months.

I now had the monies necessary for printing. I would worry about the separate binding costs at a later date. I felt that the book needed the name of a known Jewish publisher rather than a fabricated logo. At the time, I was a music teacher in an afternoon Hebrew school, and among my students were the children of the owners of Bloch Publishing Company. The Bloch name was recognized throughout the Jewish community in the United States and Canada as a distinguished publisher of Judaica. The owner agreed to let me use the Bloch Company logo in exchange for a distribution fee on those books sold by his company. Since he would claim no monies outside this fee, I felt that this was equitable.

While the book was on press, I received a telephone call from a family in Amsterdam, New York who were in need of sheet music for their daughter's forthcoming wedding. I arranged with my printer to have one set of pre-bound sheets folded and sent immediately to the family. Yet another *mitzvah*, I was told. I borrowed additional funds from family so that the books could be bound. The pre-publication orders were delivered within the time promised. I then contacted a number of Judaica shops around the country and placed several copies, on consignment, in their stores. The book was, of course, not a "best seller." Eventually, *Songs of the Hasidim* became known primarily through purchasers' recommendations.

On the merit of my work, I received a research grant in 1969, from the Memorial Foundation for Jewish Culture. Personal savings, small grants, and sabbaticals from two schools, in which I served as music director, afforded me the opportunity to go with my family to Israel for additional research and collection. By means of extended interviews, *farbrengen* and other occasions when I could use electronic equipment, I recorded hundreds of *nigunim* and background information from my hasidic advisors and informants. Back home in my studio in the sleepy little town of Kiryat Ono, I transcribed the melodies and edited the information. In 1971, less than a year after our return to the United States, *Songs of the Hasidim Volume II* was published. Like *Songs of the Hasidim*, this second volume also bore the imprint of the Bloch Publishing Company.

In 1972, the idea came to me that an inexpensively priced paperback edition, featuring the best-known songs from the two hardbound volumes, might bring this material to a broader public. Accordingly, my wife and I spent the better part of our evenings in summer camp, re-cutting and re-pasting from the original books and preparing galleys for an overview collection of 125 songs. Along the way, we also decided to issue an edition with a special thematic music guide to assist club-date musicians in locating their customers' requested songs more easily. The set-up for both books, *Hasidic Favorites* and *Hasidic-Israeli Club Date*, was finished during the summer. Looking for a publishing company name, I decided to drop the opening *A* from my youngest daughter's, name, and Tara Publications was born. In the beginning, I received quizzical looks because Tara sounded Irish, and many remembered the well-known Tara from the movie, *Gone With the Wind*. "Why this name for a Jewish company?" several asked. When my wife found that, according to legend, the grandaughter of King David brought a Tara (Irish pronunciation for Torah) to Ireland, we were able to give this, in addition to Atara, as a reason for the company name.

Under the Tara Publication banner we have succeeded in publishing and distributing more than 200 books which include the broad panorama of Jewish music—Hasidic, Israeli, Yiddish, Sephardic, Ladino, Oriental, Klezmer, Cantorial, Instrumental, Art Songs, Choral and Children's music. In addition, several thousand recordings in compact disk and cassette format as well as music videos are regularly distributed to Judaica stores throughout North America. Our broad-based music catalogue and Internet site on the worldwide web have made Jewish music available to interested individuals and institutions throughout the world.

It has been a long, but rewarding trip, since my father's *zmirot*.

"Were I blessed with a sweet voice, I could sing you new hymns and songs every day, for with the daily rejuvenation of the world, new songs are created."

—Rabbi of Ger

"DON'T CONDUCT"
THE LUBAVITCH RECORDING

In 1962, I was approached by Benedict Stambler, a collector of Jewish music and a pioneer in the field of hasidic recordings in the United States, to arrange and conduct a chorus of Lubavitch Hasidim for the first in a series of Chabad recordings. Rabbi Shmuel Zalmanoff, editor of both volumes of *Sefer Hanigunim* (books of transcribed Lubavitch nigunim) was appointed music consultant for this recording. He selected the songs and chose the Lubavitch Hasidim who were to sing in the chorus. Neither Stambler nor I had anything to do with the selection process. This was the "hand-picked chorus" I would train and record.

At our first meeting, a copy of *Sefer Hanigunim* was given to me and I was asked to play while the group sang through the program of melodies to be recorded. Because these hasidim sang so many of the songs differently from the printed musical transcriptions, I found it necessary to rewrite most of the *nigunim*. Correct transcriptions were necessary for the backup singers and instrumental ensemble that would accompany the hasidim. After the printed *nigunim* were corrected, I set about to arrange them with simple harmonies.

Our first rehearsal, took place in a basement in Crown Heights, and I was forced to quickly address an interesting problem. My rather forthright instruction that the chorus must begin and end together, was met with very quizzical looks. "Hasidim always begin and end together," they objected. It took me a little time to realize that the members of my chorus did most of their singing during *farbrengen* (special hasidic gatherings), which took place several times a year at Lubavitch headquarters. The format of a Lubavitch *farbrengen* was constant. Hundreds of hasidim gathered in Lubavitch headquarters at 770 Eastern Parkway, in Brooklyn, and for several hours listened raptly to a discourse by Rabbi Menachem Mendl Schneerson, the Lubavitcher Rebbe, punctuated at various times with the singing of *nigunim* by the entire gathering. A designated hasid, who took his cue when the Rebbe motioned with his hand, began a *nigun* that was taken up by all assembled. The singing ended abruptly when the Rebbe motioned once again. Every eye focused on the Rebbe as he continued the discourse.

For a young conductor to inform these singers that they needed to start together and end together served only to insult them. It took great effort to convince them that a taped recording of a *farbrengen* would prove beyond doubt, that the beginnings and endings of the *nigunim* were ragged and far below the musical standards needed for a professional recording. When they finally agreed, I had my first empiric victory.

After several months of weekly rehearsals, during which they learned to watch my hands, sing *legato*, and produce some elementary shadings of tone, I found that, try as they might, none of the hasidim were able to sing the harmonies that I had written. This was not due to their level of difficulty, but for the hasidim to concentrate on anything but the melody seemed almost impossible. With permission from Lubavitch, I hired three "ringers" (professionals) to sing the harmonies. The rehearsals went well, and after several months, when I felt that I had taken the group musically as far as it could go, I asked that a recording date be scheduled.

I was told that the recording session must take place either on Monday evening after dark or on Tuesday before dark. This was in keeping with the belief among traditional Jews that Tuesday, the third day of the week, is a day of *mazel* (good luck). In the Book of Genesis, it is written that God looked out each day and "saw that it was good." Only on the third day are the words "saw that it was good" repeated a second time. Tuesday, therefore, became a "doubly good" (lucky) day. Whenever possible, Jews choose Tuesday to announce an engagement, move to a new house or apartment, hold a wedding ceremony, open a new business etc., all in the belief that this day holds good luck for those endeavors. It was, therefore, in keeping with this idea that the Lubavitch Hasidim requested that their first recording session be held on a Tuesday, the day of good luck. According to the Jewish calendar, a new day begins with the preceding evening, Monday after dark is considered to be Tuesday. The producers promised that they would schedule a recording studio and an engineer for Tuesday. When a studio was obtained, a final recording date (a Monday night in early Spring) was announced. Rabbi Zalmanoff instructed us that on the Saturday night before the recording, we were to gather for a "mini-*farbrengen*." When I asked the reason, I was told, that as hasidim performing a task for Lubavitch, they needed an evening of good fellowship in which to wish each other luck with the recording. Dutifully, the producers and I arrived at the home of one of the singers an hour after Shabbos was over. Upon entering, we found tables filled with refreshments, drink, and spirits. For the first time since the rehearsals began, I was afforded the opportunity of listening to each of my hasidim sing solo. Some of them, on the merit of their vocal abilities, would never have been permitted to sing in any chorus. At the end of the evening, however, we left full of good cheer and spurred on to the forthcoming Lubavitch recording.

The producers had been able to rent a studio on Eighth Avenue near 57th Street in New York City. A well-known sound engineer, David Hancock, was engaged. Hancock had been one of the first sound engineers to transfer old, seventy-eight r.p.m. recordings of the great cantors of the 20th century to magnetic tape for the Collectors Guild Record Company. In the process, much of the static and other extraneous noises were eliminated. Through this rather tedious and time-consuming work, Hancock, who was not Jewish, became very familiar with and developed great fondness for Hebrew liturgical music. He looked forward to a live recording session of hasidic music. His admonition to me was to get the "Lubos" (his endearing term for the hasidim) into the studio no later than 7:30 p.m. At the then going rate of $45.00 per hour, the studio was quite expensive. I made sure that each of my singers and "ringers" knew the cost and importance of being on time.

I arrived at the studio by 6:30 p.m., discussed microphone set up with our engineer, arranged placement of the chorus and instrumentalists, and set the order in which the selections would be recorded. At 7:20 p.m. Hancock asked, "Where are they?" Looking for my singers, I opened the window onto Eighth Avenue. The location of this studio was a center of Rock 'n Roll music and the area was full of hippies, many of whom wore beards. To locate my bearded hasidim was like looking for a needle in a haystack. At 7:25, I repeated the action and placed my head far out the window in order to get a better view of the street. This time I saw what looked like my hasidim about a block away. As they approached, I noticed that there were far too many of them. I could only assume that my singers had encountered another group of hasidim in the subway and they were walking together up Eighth Avenue. I believed that at the entrance to the studio the group would split, and my hasidim would enter the building while the others continued to their destination. Was I wrong! After the fifth elevator disgorged itself, there were more than sixty people in the studio. Only twenty-four of them belonged to my chorus and orchestra; the others were older hasidim, women, and children. Before I had a chance to vent my anger, I saw two men remove bottles of soda from a crate, and several women unfurl baked goods including honey and sponge cake. Finally, for the *piece d'resistance*, a hasid opened two brown paper bags and revealed four bottles of *"zeks und ninetsiger"* (192 proof vodka). He began to pass filled shot glasses to all the singers. I could no longer contain myself and began to shout:

"What is going on here?"

"We're going to have a *farbrengen*," one of the hasidim responded gingerly.

"Here? Now? Why?" I asked in chagrin.

The hasidim tried to calm me down. I was informed again that they were not professional singers. They could not simply approach a microphone and sing. Because they were doing the bidding of the Lubavitcher Rebbe, it was necessary for them to "warm up" both physically and spiritually. This could only be accomplished through a *farbrengen.*

"How long will this *farbrengen* last?" I asked rather timidly.

I discovered that a good question would always merit a good answer from a hasid. "This *farbrengen* will last only as long as it lasts. Not one minute longer," came the reply.

A hasid took out a photograph of the Rebbe and attached it to the wall with a thumbtack. The cake and the spirits were passed around, with soda substituted for the women and the children. Each singer toasted the Rebbe in absentia, and wished the others good luck in the duties they were about to perform. As the conductor, I was asked to join in the *l'chaim* (toast) and was given a small glass filled with vodka. Never having drunk alcohol of this strength, I imagined that the effect was similar to drinking *Draino,* the special liquid touted in commercial advertisements as "unclogging everything on its way down."

The producers and sound engineers looked on from the control room in amazement. "I don't believe this. We should get a reporter and a camera man from the entertainment newspaper *Variety* because no one will believe that this scene happened unless it is documented."

My singers and the other hasidim took their time— fifty minutes in all. When the *farbrengen* was over, the soda, the vodka and the cake were whisked away. All those not in the chorus were put on the sidelines of the studio, and my sixteen singers and three ringers stepped up to the waiting microphones. One hasid proclaimed, "Now we are ready to do the bidding of the Lubavitcher Rebbe."

I finally felt that I had control of the situation. However, just before I gave the downbeat to the orchestra, Rabbi Zalmanoff approached me.

"Before we begin I need a small favor from you," he said.

"Certainly," I replied, "what is it?"

"It's a small favor," he repeated, "Please don't conduct."

"Please what?" I asked in astonishment. "What do you mean don't conduct?"

For some reason, he must have thought that I was having trouble with his English.

"Don't make with the hands," he said. "Sit down, you'll get paid anyway."

"What do you mean sit down?" I retorted. "I spent six months of my life rehearsing this group to get them ready for this recording and now you tell me not to conduct? Please, tell me —what is the problem?"

"I see that you are a difficult man, so I will tell you the truth. You can conduct, but nobody will watch you."

"Why will they not watch me?" I asked in almost total desperation.

"Because if they watch you, it will get in the way of their *kavanah* (concentration)," he replied.

There it was, out in the open. I moved toward the chorus, and gave the downbeat. The instrumentalists picked up the introduction while sixteen pairs of eyes closed on me. I could have been in another state as far as my singers were concerned. They sang with joy and fervor and the entire studio was permeated with the intensity of their singing. I realized that, at the very least, I had prepared them well enough to be able to sing their own melody and keep in time with the instrumentalists.

Thus began our recording session. We moved along briskly until approximately ten o' clock when an unexpected situation took place. Like most recording studios, ours had a light outside its door. Since any movement or noise can be picked up by the sophisticated recording equipment, the sound engineer would turn on the light when actual recording rather than rehearsing took place. It is the rule in all recording establishments that when this light is on, one does not move around, enter or exit the studio. We began rehearsing the well-known *Uforatsto* (see page 98).

God in his celestial abode often creates truly interesting *shiduchim* (matches) on earth below. Our main recording studio was attached to a secondary studio, which had access to the hallway and restrooms only through ours. The smaller studio had been rented for the evening to a group of ballet dancers who rehearsed clad in skintight leotards. One of the young female dancers, needing to use the outside facilities, and noting that the recording light was not on, quietly entered the main studio and made her way to the hallway. Because I was busy conducting the instrumentalists, I did not notice her, nor did I see what transpired in the room. Suddenly, I was brought up short by a cry of "cut" from the control booth. I looked up and found that my singers had disappeared.

"Where are they?" I shouted.

No one seemed to know. I ran into the hallway but found it empty. I quickly took the elevator down to the street level. Outside, on Eighth Avenue, I found my Lubavitch chorus.

"What are you doing out here?" I asked trying to restrain myself.

"You did not see what happened up there in the studio?"

"What happened?" I asked.

"A girl in almost no clothing came into the room as we were singing *Ufaratsta,* they replied.

"So?" I asked in bewilderment.

"So we left," said the hasid.

"So you left?" I said trying to control myself.

"Yes!" the hasid replied. You see, Rabbi Pasternak (hasidim sometimes give honorary ordination to people who work for them, and although I did not have a degree in rabbinics, I was nevertheless awarded the title), you do not understand who we are. Suppose for a moment that we were in the middle of prayers in the synagogue and a scantily dressed woman walked in. What would we do? We would simply close our prayer books and leave the synagogue. The same thing is true here. You have thought of us all along as a group of singers. The truth of the matter is that we are not singers; we are hasidim here to do the bidding of the Lubavitcher Rebbe. For us this recording is similar to a worship service. So, in a situation like this, we must do exactly what we would do in a synagogue."

I felt the blood rush to my head. I said to them in disbelief:

"The age of miracles is not past. I, who had my eyes open, did not see the scantily clad girl enter the room, but you, who had your eyes closed, were able to see her?"

"All right Rabbi, no jokes."

"Okay, it's over. Let's get back to the recording," I responded.

I was told that, unless the dancers were moved to another studio, my singers would not return.

"How am I to change their studio?" I asked.

"You are a bright man. We're sure that you will find a way."

I took the elevator up to the office and looked for the manager.

"We must change the studio of the ballet dancers," I said.

"Impossible!" said the manager.

"Do you know who my people are?" I asked.

"No, and frankly I don't care ," replied the manager

"They are a group of Amish from Lancaster, Pennsylvania and they are here with their spiritual leader to record their music," I explained. "And if they can't finish tonight, it will be a financial and spiritual disaster for them." The manager hesitated. After all, for Amish one should have respect even if one does not fully understand their lifestyle. He was thoroughly convinced, however, when I offered him the remains of the bottle of 192 proof vodka. While I went to get the bottle, the manager changed the room for the dancers.

There is an expression in Yiddish, *"Men lacht mit yashrishkes"* (loosely translated as, "you laugh on the outside but with heartache on the inside"). Although when looking back it seems quite comical, it was not funny when it happened. To the tribute of the Lubavitch Hasidim, they were right and I was wrong. These were handpicked hasidim, instructed to present to the world the first recorded music of Lubavitch, at the bidding of the Rebbe. As such, they treated the project with much more religious conviction and feeling than I had.

Bad singers come in a number of varieties. Among these are singers who sing flat (pull down from the tone), and those who sing sharp (overbound the tone). Given the choice of teaching either of these singers, a vocal coach would probably choose the one that sings sharp. He might conclude that this singer, in an attempt to reach the correct tone, moves above it, whereas the singer who sings flat is not aiming at all.

During the Lubavitch recording session described above, a major problem could not be resolved. When the hasidim sang three *dvekus* melodies attributed to the first Rebbe of Lubavitch, in each song the pitch began to rise—a quarter tone, a half tone, and finally a full tone. In music, this is quite a distance. Because they were untrained singers, I assumed that they were not hearing the instrumentalists who were positioned in front of them. The solution, I thought, would be to take the musicians playing portable instruments and place them close to the hasidim. I placed the violinist, clarinetist, trumpeter, and flautist each between two Lubavitch singers, so that the the instruments were only several inches from their ears. For a few moments the singing was steady, but soon it again began to rise. No matter how many times we tried, the results were the same. I finally came to the realization that, although the hasidim were ostensibly singing these songs for me, their conductor, they were really directing their songs to God in heaven on high. As they strove to get the melody heavenward, the pitch kept rising.

The recording of these three songs could not be salvaged. Consequently, several weeks later, the hasidim were brought back to the studio to record the songs a cappella. After they left, the sound engineer overdubbed an accordion accompaniment to the vocals. When the pitch of the singers began to rise, the engineer adjusted the recorded speed of the accordion to match the pitch of the Lubavitcher hasidim. Thankfully, the songs were saved and became part of the recording. When it was released, a critical review in the *London Jewish Chronicle* proclaimed this to be one of the finest authentic Jewish recordings ever made.

Several months after this recording was issued, the producers received a call from Leonard Bernstein's office in New York City. They were told that the world famous conductor had come across the Lubvitcher recording and wanted to use one of the selections for a program of religious folk music. Truly flattered and at the same time awed by the knowledge that this great musician would even listen to a recording of hasidic music, they gave permission. Forty years later, their embarrasment can be revealed. Yes, the selection was played —on Christmas eve which happened in that year to fall on a Friday night.

"Speech reveals the thought of the mind, but melody reveals the emotions of longing and delight. These stem from the inner self, from the very soul, and are much higher than reason and intellect."

—Sayings of Chabad

"DON'T WORRY, DO IT"
BOBOV RECORDING

In 1962, Benedict Stambler, of the Collectors Guild Recording Company, and I were invited to meet with the Bobover Rebbe in his Brooklyn residence. During our conversation, the Rebbe related that he had been perturbed when his young son brought home a melody that he had learned in his yeshiva. When the child was asked if he realized that the song had been composed by his paternal grandfather, the boy shook his head. Turning to us, the Rebbe said, "If my own child does not know the origins of our *nigunim* how can I expect my hasidim and their children to know? Would the two of you be willing to help correct this situation and undertake a project of documenting and preserving our music on a phonograph recording?" he asked. " In this way, our own hasidim, as well as other Jews, will know the music of their heritage. When we accepted, the Rebbe told us that the mechanics and production of the recording would be left to us, but for the sake of Bobov and musical accuracy, we were to work closely with his knowledgeable relative, Rabbi Laizer Halberstam. Reb Laizer (as we began to refer to him) would not only be the musical adviser, but he would also serve as the soloist for the recording.

Several days later, we met with Reb Laizer and, during the course of several hours, decided on the selections to be recorded. No Bobover nigunim appeared in print at that time and it was therefore necessary to transcribe them in music notation. Reb Laizer sang them into a tape recorder so that I could write them down at my leisure. Before he began, he informed me that he would sing them in "the authentic way." When I did not quite grasp his meaning, he explained that he would sing with the pronunciation of the hasidim who lived in Poland.

After the mass emigration of Jews from Europe to America in the 20th century, Lithuanian was the standard pronunciation for both Yiddish and Hebrew. When the State of Israel was established in 1948, Sephardic became the official pronunciation in the Holy Land and it was exported to synagogues and educational institutions throughout the world. Reb Laizer explained that recording with either of these pronunciations would be unacceptable, and they must be sung with the pronunciation used in Bobov. Although I had not yet digested the ramifications of this order, I assured Reb Laizer that I would comply with his wishes.

Several evenings later Rabbi Halberstam brought to my home a tape recording with fourteen songs, and I began transcribing the melodies. Once they were written down, I had to solve the problem of writing the Hebrew lyrics beneath the melody line. Music notes on staff lines are sung or played from left to right, but Hebrew is read from right to left. Consequently, if one writes Hebrew letters underneath the notes, not only does the Hebrew appear backward, but also the syllables within the words themselves move backwards.

In Palestine, during the early part of the 20th century, music transcribers were aware that this was a problem for music readers in other parts of the world. In a bold but quite clever stroke, these innovative Jewish musicians solved the problem by simply putting the treble clef on the right side of the staff and writing the notes from right to left. By adjusting the left right movement of the music, the Hebrew followed beneath the notes in correct fashion. How simple and wonderful! Editions of "backward" Jewish music were issued and can be found to this day in libraries and private collections. Unfortunately, for those trained to sing or play from music in the standard left to right mode, encountering music moving in the opposite direction is, to say the least, disconcerting. Musicians outside of Palestine devised a less awkward solution by using transliterations with English letters. Now notes and lyrics were read in the same direction. Ever since then, with the exception of Israel, most Jewish music lyrics appear in transliterated form.

If I were to transliterate the blessing recited before drinking wine in the Lithuanian pronunciation scheme, I would write, *Bo-ruch A-to Ado-noy Elo-he-nu me-lech ho-o-lom bo-re pri hago-fen*

In Sephardic pronunciation, I would have written, *Ba-ruch A-ta Ado-nai Elo-he-nu me-lech Ha-o-lam bo-re pri ha-ga-fen*

In the Bobover pronunciation, however, I was forced to write, *Boor-yech A-too Ado-noy Eloy-hay-nee may-lech hoo-oy-lom bo-ray pri ha-goo-fen*

I looked at my first line of Bobover transliteration. "Impossible," I shouted and ran to the telephone. When Reb Laizer answered, I greeted him with a rush.

"Rabbi, I know that you want to be authentic, but to sing with this pronunciation is to destroy the sales potential of the recording."

"How do you know that?" he asked.

"Most of your sales will be to non-hasidim who will be interested in this music as part of Jewish culture."

"What makes you think that real hasidim will not buy?" he retorted.

"All I know is that I have been to hasidic homes and many don't have phonograph turntables that revolve at the correct speed."

"You are wrong! You are wrong!" he said. "Besides, this is Bobov and it must be done authentic. Don't worry! Don't worry! Do it!"

I hung up the telephone and returned to the transliterations, which I finished the following week. Some of the transliterations were not easy for me to look at, and several times, when I was almost ready to throw my hands up in total frustration, I called Reb Laizer. Each time I heard the same comforting words, "Don't worry, do it." So I did it!

The music was prepared and it was now time to form a chorus and engage instrumentalists for the recording. Having had rather difficult experience in the past with hasidic singers, I opted for professionals. I decided to use cantors as a "hasidic chorus," assuming that professionals, who had strong Judaic as well as musical background, would be able to sing hasidic melodies with unusual sounding lyrics. It was understood that the members of the Hasidic Chorale would be paid a minimum. The cantors agreed that their primary rewards would be the fellowship and joy that comes from singing together, while at the same time preserving a musical heritage threatened to be lost.

The producers planned two rehearsals before the recording session, one with the chorale only, and the second together with the accompanying instrumental ensemble. The first rehearsal was held in a rented hall on 57th Street in New York City. Reb Laizer arrived and soon thereafter the sixteen members of the chorale, who were introduced to him and to each other. I had photocopied sets of music, which I placed on a stand for each singer. By chance, the song *Simon Tov* was the first selection in each music folder. The song, with words from the *Melave Malke* liturgy, was extremely popular in Bobov, and was sung at weddings, bar mitzvahs, and other happy occasions. In the Lithuanian pronunciation scheme the transliteration would have appeared as,

Si-mon tov u-mazl tov y'-he lo-nu u-l'chol yis-ro-el o-men.
In the Bobov pronunciation however, I had transliterated in the following manner, *Sim-en toyv ee-mazl toyv y'-hay loo-nee ee-l'-chol yis-ru-ayl oo-mayn.* I told the members of the chorus to pick up the first song sheet. Although I expected some comments from the group about the pronunciation, I was taken back by the first question.

"So, Velvel, in what language are we singing tonight?" After a rather pregnant pause, I replied, "This recording is going to be made using the pronunciation of the Bobover Hasidim. I have been through this with the Rabbi and it is his very strong conviction that this material must be preserved in the most authentic manner and with **this** Hebrew and Yiddish pronunciation."

The members of the chorale nodded their heads in understanding. I gave the downbeat and we were on our way. The opening words *simen toyv* offered no problems. The next phrase, *ee-mazl toyv* was also fine. As soon as they sang the words *y'hay loo-nee*, several members began to snicker.

"What's the problem? " I asked.

"*Y-'hay loo-nee* sounds like looney tunes," said one of the younger members of the group.

"Come on now," I said, "let's try it again."

Once again *y'-hay loo-nee* brought the singing to a stop. We tried it again and again, but the laughter continued. I put down my baton and walked over to Reb Laizer.

"You see, I was right," I said. "If these professional cantors can't get through this pronunciation, what will the rest of the Jewish world do?"

"Don't worry," he said. "Go back!"

I returned to the conductor's stand and said, "Gentlemen let's try it again." As will happen, when laughter begins, it often feeds on itself. *Y'hay loo-nee* stopped us each time.

"Velvel," said one of the singers, "we'll take care of it."

The cantors put down their music and walked over to Reb Laizer. He was a large, imposing man, meticulously dressed in a *capote* (frock coat) and an oversized black hat. As the cantors approached, he folded his arms across his chest. Everyone seemed to be talking at once.

"Rabbi, it sounds very funny to say *y'-hay loo-nee*. We know the words to this song and can sing them with 'normal' pronunciation. The way we have been singing is ridiculous."

Reb Laizer, with a marvelous twinkle in his eye, waited until the talking died down and then said gently, in accented but quite good English,

"Everybody said what they wanted to say? Everyone is finished with suggestions?"

The cantors nodded.

"Now I want to tell you and your fancy conductor a story. You see when a *choosid* (his pronunciation) sees that he can't convince people in the normal way, he tells them a story. Therefore, I will tell you a story."

The cantors moved a little closer to listen to Reb Laizer and his tale. After all these years, I still cannot, in all honesty, believe that the story he told was created there in the recording studio. He must have had it tucked away in some readied story bag, to be brought out when he needed to hammer home the idea of authenticity. To my mind I have never found a better story to convey the importance of ethnicity or authenticity. Reb Laizer began:

"A group of *tensers* [dancers] from the Ivory Coast and their cultural minister approached the cultural minister of Israel and said:

'We would like to have intercultural relations between our two countries. Therefore, we will send you our *tensers* from the Ivory Coast to perform in Israel, and you in turn will send your artists to perform in the Ivory Coast.'

'That would be wonderful,' said the cultural minister of Israel. 'It will truly help our inter-cultural relations.'

'Before we come to Israel,' said the Ivory Coast minister, 'we must make you aware of a small problem.'

'Problem?' said the Israeli minister, 'what problem?'

'You see in the Ivory Coast our *tensers* perform only *barechested.*'

'Only *barechested?*' said the Israeli minister, 'what does this mean?'

The Ivory Coast minister raised his hands to the neck area and brought them slowly down to his waist. 'From up there to down here—nothing!'

"You really mean open, exposed, *nakid* [Yiddish for naked] really bare chested?' said the ruffled Israeli minister. 'You know what will happen to me if you bring *barechested tensers* to Israel? The chief rabbi in Jerusalem will put me over a cliff and everyone will throw stones at me. The chief rabbi in Tel Aviv will hang me from a light pole and everyone who passes by will kick me. Why can't you bring me normal *tensers* so that we can keep intercultural relations?'

Suddenly the minister from Israel smiled. 'Sha, sha,' he said. 'No problem, no problem. You can bring your *tensers* to Israel. When you land in Lod Airport, we will have a welcoming committee who will present your *tensers* with some *shmattes* [literally rags, but here meaning fabric that may be used as halters]. You will simply put these *shmattes* on and cover **it** up. (And Reb Laizer pointed to his chest and made a broad expansive circle with his hands.)

'Cover it up? Cover it up?' said the minister from the Ivory Coast in disbelief. 'If we cover it up,' he said, 'they will no longer be the *tensers* from the Ivory Coast. Maybe *tensers* from some other part of Africa. But the *tensers* from the Ivory Coast can only *tense* open, exposed, *nakid*, and *barechested*.'

Reb Laizer smiled contentedly at the conclusion of his story and was ready to drive his point home.

"The same is with you and your fancy conductor," said Reb Laizer. "You are all embarrassed when you sing *y'-hay loo-nee.* It sounds so open, so exposed, so *nakid*, so *barechested*. Therefore, you would like to take a little Lithuanian *shmatte* and cover it up so that the words become *y'-hey lo-nu*" (he seemed to enjoy mimicking the sound). "Therefore, I tell you simply, that if you cover up this pronunciation, *Simon Tov* will no longer be a song of the Bobover Hasidim. Our music must be open, exposed, *nakid*, and *barechested*, without any shame. And now I ask you and your fancy conductor to go back to your seats and sing *y'-hay loo-nee* and all the *barechested* pronunciations until you *platz* (explode)."

Sixteen members of the chorus and their "fancy conductor" sheepishly walked back to their seats. One of the cantors said,

"Velvel, if that man, with that beard, that capote, that black hat, could tell us that story in order to convince us of authenticity, then we are absolutely going to sing it for him in the way that he wants."

The group settled down, and began to sing, *y'-hay loo-nee* and all other "deviant" pronunciations without a snicker. The truth is, Reb Laizer was right, and I, the "fancy conductor" and my chorus were wrong. He had the passionate feeling that preserving the authenticity of this hasidic repertoire was primary. To his lasting memory, the two recordings of Bobov, issued under his guidance, rang true. Many hasidim as well as the broad-based Jewish public, saw these recordings as a true musical documentation of one of the important hasidic dynasties.

For many years after the Bobov recordings, my company, Tara Publications, exhibited musical materials at the annual convention of the Cantors Assembly of America. Each spring, several hundred cantors gathered at the popular Grossingers Resort in Liberty, New York. Invariably, cantors, who had been members of the Bobover Chorale, arriving at our exhibit, would greet us with the now beloved *y'-hay loo-nee*. This phrase served us as a momento of several incredible evenings recording and preserving a glorious heritage of hasidic song.

Rejoice that you have an opportunity to sing unto God."
—Rabbi Mendel of Vitebsk

MUSIC IN THE RAW

The first recordings of Modzitz, released in the late 1950s, were followed by those of Bobov, Ger, Vishnitz and other hasidic courts. Vladimir Heifetz, a graduate of the Russian Conservatory in St. Petersburg, and a former accompanist for the famed Russian singer, Feodor Chaliapin, provided orchestrations for several of these recordings. Heifetz, a secular Jew, emigrated to the United States from Russia in 1921, and after scoring music for a number of films, found permanent work through the Workmen's Circle in New York City. He became totally involved in Jewish music, both Yiddish and liturgical, and was highly sought out as an arranger, pianist and conductor.

In the early recordings, I arranged the choral settings, and Heifetz based his orchestrations on these arrangements. After these recordings were released, he asked where he could hear hasidic music "in the raw." He complained that he had never heard *nigunim* as they were sung by the hasidim themselves, but had to content himself by getting them "second hand" from me and the chorus of cantors we had formed for the recordings. He felt that he could better understand this music were he to hear it directly from the hasidim.

I told him that he was right and that his request was timely, for *Simchas Torah*, one of the most joyous festivals of the year featuring the *Hakofos* (Procession of Torah Scrolls), would take place in three weeks. During this festival, in synagogues all over the world, Jews spend the night singing and dancing with the Torahs. I gave him the date, time and addresses of two large synagogues in Brooklyn, one of Hungarian and the other of Russian hasidim. I guaranteed him that, in both these synagogues, *Hakofos* would provide him with music "in the raw."

Several weeks later I met him, and he reported on his *Simchas Torah* experience. On the evening of the festival, he dressed in a light colored suit, put a white *kipa* (skullcap) into his pocket and hailed a cab to the Williamsburgh section of Brooklyn. He arrived at the first synagogue and found the *Hakofos* in full force. Upon entering, he realized that he was the only person in the room not dressed in black clothing, and that his white *kipa* was unique to this gathering. He therefore positioned himself in the rear of the synagogue where he felt that he would be as unobtrusive as possible.

He watched the hasidim dancing joyously with the Torahs held aloft and listened carefully to their singing. He found that his body began to move in rhythm to the music. Soon he was particularly taken with a melody and, fully prepared, he removed music staff paper from his breast pocket, and began to transcribe the melody. No sooner had he finished the first line than two hasidim escorted him to the doorway. Without saying a word, they walked him gently down the stairs to the street where they wished him good night and took leave of him. He was unsure of the reason for his eviction and he was certainly unaware, at this point in time, that music writing or any other writing, was prohibited among traditional Jews on a Sabbath or festival. Undaunted, he hailed a passing cab and asked to be taken to a synagogue in another section of Brooklyn. Upon entering the main Lubavitch synagogue at 770 Eastern Parkway, in the Crown Heights section of Brooklyn, Heifetz found that the proceedings were still in the early stages. He remained in the rear, listened and watched with a great deal of interest. He was quite intrigued with the energy and fervor of the hasidim as they sang and danced. Suddenly, a melody that he found musically interesting was introduced. Again the sheet of manuscript paper came out of his breast pocket, and he began transcribing the *nigun*. When he had finished the transcription and the staff paper was back in his pocket, he was approached by a hasid with the words *sholom alechem*, the traditional Jewish greeting of welcome. After discovering the nature of Heifetz's visit, the hasid gently told him that writing on Sabbath or festivals was prohibited. The hasid realized that Heifetz's transgression had not been committed willfully and did not pursue the matter further. He introduced Heifetz to other hasidim who made him feel truly welcome.

Seeing and hearing the hasidim sing in their natural habitats made Heifetz better understand their music, and in later recordings he was able to create arrangements that were more in consonance with the style of the hasidic folksongs. Having experienced hasidic music first hand rather than from me, a secondary source, he was able to internalize the melodies and give the arrangements more of a Jewish rather than the Russian flavor which had been evident in his earlier recordings.

"Song opens a window to the secret places of the soul."

—Sayings of Chabad

HASIDIC DANCE
In Ritual and Celebration

To most people, all hasidic dancing by males may look similar. There seems to be little difference in the dancing styles of Polish, Russian or Hungarian hasidim. An in-depth study of hasidic dance, however, disproved this notion, and brought many differences to light.

In the 1970s, Jill Gellerman, a young lady raised in Iowa, was pursuing a graduate degree in dance at a mid-western university. Before beginning her course of studies, she vacationed in Israel and, while visiting the Western Wall, befriended a young lady from Brooklyn. Because both women were returning to the United States before the *Sukot* festival, Gellerman was invited to spend *Simchas Torah* in Brooklyn with her new found friend. On the eve of *Shmini Atseret*, the seventh day of *Sukot*, Gellerman was taken to a hasidic *shtibel*. There, as in all hasidic synagogues, *Hakofos* take place both on this night and the following evening and morning of *Simchas Torah*. From behind the *mechitza*, Gellerman could see, although with some difficulty, men dancing ecstatically. After receiving explanation from her host, Gellerman understood what she was witnessing. Intrigued, Gellerman asked if it was possible to see dancing by other hasidim, and over the next forty-eight hours she was taken to some of the major hasidic synagogues in Brooklyn.

Immediately after the holiday, Gellerman returned to her dance studies. Because she had been so affected by what she had seen in Brooklyn, she approached her professors and requested permission to change the focus of her dissertation. After explaining hasidim and her interest in their dance, her thesis change was approved. Towards the end of her course work, she called me, and among other things thanked me for my book, *Songs of the Hasidim*, which she had found useful while writing her dissertation. At the same time she informed me, that, with the encouragement of her professors, she had submitted a grant proposal for a study in hasidic dance to the National Endowment in Washington, D.C. She asked if I would accept the position of music consultant for the project. I could not help but recall my frustration in the late 1960s in attempting to get funding for my hasidic book project. I was convinced that hasidic dancing would not be high on the priority list of the National Endowment. I felt that to say so would be discouraging to Gellerman, so I accepted her offer to be the music consultant. Several months later she called to tell me that it "looked good." I still could not see government money being given for such a project. Shortly thereafter, however, her joyous phone call proved how wrong I was. Gellerman was awarded a sizable grant for, *Hasidic Dance in Ritual and Celebration*, focusing on hasidim from Polish, Russian and Hungarian backgrounds.

Gellerman felt that videotaping hasidim dancing would be the most efficient way to begin the documentation process. After she received refusals by a number of hasidic groups, I used my position as arranger and conductor for the recordings of Bobov to gain entrée for Gellerman and her video camera. She was given permission to videotape, through an opening in the *mechitza* curtain, at the annual Bobov Purim festivities. Although Gellerman could barely be seen, she caught several angry glances from hasidim. Nevertheless, it seemed that the taping would go well. Seemingly out of nowhere, an excited looking hasid attacked the video camera with a glass of water. This incident forced us to conclude that continued videotaping, especially by a woman, would only bring on additional confrontations. Sadly, she put the camera down and we both left the synagogue. Another plan of action was needed and a creative Gellerman found one.

She contacted several kosher caterers in Brooklyn and offered a free videotape to any bride and groom that would allow her to photograph their wedding. The floodgates, so to speak, opened and she had more invitations for videotaping than she could accept. Although TV is not usually found in hasidic homes, video recorders and monitors are plentiful. A videotaping of a major life event such as a wedding, however, is often not affordable for young hasidic couples, and therefore the great response to Gellerman's offer.

The shooting and editing took place over several months and each week we viewed the tapes and I transcribed the melodies that accompanied the dances. Gellerman set the labanotations (a system of dance movement transcription) and the analysis of the different movements, stresses, bodily positions etc.

I recall the grand wedding of a Rebbe, with many hundreds of hasidim in attendance. The moment Gellerman saw the bride on the dance floor she knew that the young lady was from California. Since she had no information beforehand as to the bride's hometown, I could not understand how she knew this. By the way she moved her body, Gellerman informed me, it was evident that she was raised in Los Angeles. I looked into the matter and found that Gellerman was right.

Among other things, the study showed that hasidim of Polish, Russian and Hungarian descent danced quite differently from each other. While one group danced with forcefulness, another's style was more inhibited. Certain hasidim would dance only in a tight circle while others danced in a freer, more individualistic manner.

"NINETY CENTS FOR THE BOXES"

On my return home from California at the end of August, in 1979, I found a message on my telephone answering machine from Rabbi Stephen Robbins. When I returned his call, he informed me that he was hired as a religion consultant for a Hollywood film tentatively titled *No Knife*. The central figure in the movie was a young hasidic rabbi sent by his small Polish community to a synagogue pulpit in San Francisco. The studio's wardrobe department had assigned Rabbi Robbins the task of obtaining the hasidic garb needed for the film. He scoured the Fairfax section of Los Angeles, which abounded with stores catering to the needs of its large Jewish population. He discovered, however, that hasidic clothing was not available in Los Angeles and could be obtained only in the New York City metropolitan area. Because I worked closely with hasidim, Rabbi Robins knew that I could be helpful in providing the studio's needs.

The following day, the studio wardrobe manager called and gave me the particulars; two hasidic hats, in the style worn in Poland, a *capote* (frock coat) and an overcoat. Price, he informed me, was no object. Once the samples were received, the costume designers would duplicate as many items of clothing as needed. He asked that I notify him as soon as the clothing was in my possession. Once notified, the studio would send a messenger service to pick up the articles from my home.

At the time, the central shopping area for hasidic clothing was in the Williamsburg section of Brooklyn. On a Monday morning, two weeks before the beginning of the High Holidays, without thinking carefully, I dressed in a Pierre Cardin brown checked suit, a wide brimmed brown hat complete with colorful feather, and drove to Brooklyn. It was the height of the pre-holiday shopping season, and, as I entered the narrow Selko Hat Store, I saw the proprietress assisting eight hasidim who were busily engaged in trying on hats. Although all the hats were black, I noticed several different styles. These hats, known as *biber hitlech* among the hasidim, were imported from Czechoslovakia. The manner in which I was dressed seemed to indicate to the proprietress and the hasidim that I had wandered in by mistake and would probably leave if ignored. After several minutes, noticing that I was still standing in the rear, she called out, "For what I can do for you mister."

I approached her at the counter and in my very best English said,

"I am interested in purchasing Polish type *biber* hats. Could you please tell me what is the cost of each?"

She looked at me quizzically and replied, "Forty-seven dollars each."

I am sure that she thought the price would turn me off.

"I would like to see a Polish style *biber* hat in size seven and also in size seven and a quarter" (the studio had asked for a second hat needed for the understudy).

Again she gave me a strange look but went up a ladder and brought down two boxes. By this time, I had caught the attention of the hasidim. With large grins, they left an open path to the mirror, and placing myself squarely in front of it, I removed one of the hats from its box.

Aside from the ludicrous picture I must have created by trying on a *biber* hat while wearing a Pierre Cardin brown checked suit, neither hat was my size. There I was in front of the mirror with a small, black, *biber* hat sitting uncomfortably on my head. After placing the second hat on my head, I returned to the counter and said, "I will take them both."

The proprietress looked stunned. I took out ninety-four dollars, placed them on the counter and requested that the hats be boxed well. As she tied the boxes, her curiosity could no longer be contained.

"Mr.," she said, "for why you need such hats?"

In my very best English I responded, "Oh, they are needed for a Hollywood movie."

I could almost read her thoughts at that moment. She had only charged me the list price for the hats. For Hollywood, she could have tacked on a few dollars extra. What would it matter? I knew after she handed me the boxes that she was not yet quite finished. As my hand reached the door handle, I heard her small voice, "Mr., ninety cents for the boxes."

I turned back, handed her a dollar bill and told her to keep the change. I was sure that Hollywood could absorb the tip.

Several blocks down from the hat store, I found Broadway Clothing, an establishment which featured New York's largest collection of hasidic clothing. I told the proprietor not to ask for an explanation, but simply to sell me a *capote* and an overcoat in the sizes I needed. This was accomplished quite quickly, and, for the sum of six hundred dollars, I returned to Long Island with two *biber* hats, an elegant *capote* and a well-made overcoat. I contacted the wardrobe department, and, within four hours, a messenger service arrived at my door. Two hours later, the clothing was on a plane to California. Two days later, I found a check in my mailbox for the cost of the clothing plus a respectable addition for my services rendered.

While the film was being shot, I had the opportunity to answer several questions about hasidim that others could not answer. I responded to such queries as, "Mr. Pasternak, is it proper for a hasid to wear a *shtreimel* while traveling across the Rockies on a horse?" In addition, I gave Hollywood two pieces of unsolicited advice. It was not realistic, I informed the studio, that a hasidic rabbi, or any Orthodox rabbi for that matter, would dance with his future bride in public. I also advised them that, in keeping with the subject of the film, the music score should, at the very least, have some elements of hasidic or East European Jewish motifs. Both of my suggestions were ignored. In the final scene, the rabbi danced with his bride- to- be, and the music was in lush Hollywood style. Before release, the movie was renamed, *The Frisco Kid*, and there was the star, Gene Wilder, in the hasidic clothing that I had purchased in Brooklyn.

Maestoso

Prelude & Historical Overview

From the dawn of Creation, music was an integral part of Jewish life. Already at the beginning of Genesis, music is noted: "And his brother's name was Yuval, he was the father of all who handle the lyre and the pipe." Music, according to Jewish tradition, is thus a most ancient art and occupation. When the patriarch Jacob and his family left the house of Laban, his father-in-law complained, "Why did you flee away secretly and rob me, and did not tell me, that I might have sent you away with mirth and with songs, with tabret and lyre?" The joyous escort mentioned here is an indication that, already in the time of the patriarchs, music accompanied the cheerful events of life. Although Laban was a Syrian, the lifestyle of neighboring peoples was practically identical.

Music was used as an accompaniment to historic and national events. At the Exodus from Egypt, the Bible states, "Then sang Moses and the children of Israel this song to the Lord." After the Israelites were safely on dry land, Miriam, the sister of Moses and Aaron, took a timbrel in her hand, and all the women followed with timbrels and with dancing. Here, for the first time, instrumental accompaniment to song is noted. Following forty years of wandering in the desert, the Israelites reached their Promised Land and established themselves as a nation within their homeland. Generations later they erected their holy Temple and established the musical practices for their religious worship. Although the possibility of hearing music from Temple times does not exist, one can imagine, from descriptions given in the Talmud, that the services were grand, not only musically but also aesthetically.

An inventory of musical instruments used in the Temple service showed string, wind, brass and percussion. The numbers of each instrument, both minimum and maximum, were prescribed. *Nevel and Kinor* (stringed instruments), as is true later on in Western art music, were the predominant instruments. With regard to vocal performance in the Temple, only Levites could serve as members of the Chorus. The Levites were admitted to the Chorus at age twenty, but with a pre-requisite five year training period. After this period, they were accepted as full-fledged members. The Levites could sing in the choir until the age of fifty when they would be retired. This was in keeping with the belief at the time, that the human voice starts its downward progression at age fifty and begins to lose some of its beauty.

The vocal singing of the Levites, including the Psalm singing and the recitation of the prayers, was retained and transplanted into the *bet knesset* (the synagogue), an institution established long before the destruction of the Second Temple. The Talmud *Yerushalmi* (*Megila* 3:1) records that there were 480 synagogues in Jerusalem at the time of the Roman conquest. The *Mishna* (*Taanit* 4:2) documents the *Anshe Ma'amad*, an organization of laymen, established mainly for the purpose of transplanting the routine of Temple liturgy and music in its authentic form, to far off places. The country was divided into twenty-four sections. Twice during the year, each of these sections sent a delegate, for a period of one week, to Jerusalem. These delegates attended the Temple services, and on their return home, instructed the community in the performance of the customs, rites, and melodies according to the traditions of the Temple.

The commandment to read the Torah in public places is found in Deuteronomy. Moses commanded Israel to read the Torah at a great convocation to be held every seven years on the Feast of Tabernacles, during the time when all Israel gathered in Jerusalem. In 444 BCE, upon the return of Israel from Babylonian captivity, Ezra the Scribe read the Torah publicly in one of the open squares in Jerusalem. The tradition to read the Torah with melody was considered sacred, and was guarded and perpetuated. According to tradition, Moses brought down the Torah from Mount Sinai together with the cantillation melodies for the scriptural readings. The cantillation signs developed until the eighth century CE.

During this period, a system of accents and their representing musical and grammatical interpretation gradually evolved. The crude musical notation, which was being fashioned and perfected during the same period in the musical world at large, also influenced Jewish musical efforts in that direction. Modern day musicologists agree with the early Church fathers, that both Greek Orthodox Chant and Catholic Gregorian Chant were derived from the Temple and synagogue chants of ancient Palestine. Music history illustrates that early art music derived largely from the music of the Church. The conclusion from these historical facts is that ancient Biblical Chant served as one of the basic pillars of art music as it is known.

After the destruction of the Temple in Jerusalem, however, it seemed that music was doomed to be silenced forever within Judaism. Even before the destruction, secular music was considered a bad influence. Greek song, especially, was thought to be harmful. The spiritual leaders of Israel tried to fight against these influences by urging the people to sing only religious songs at their festive occasions. The sages challenged all singers who had sweet voices to glorify God with the gift He bestowed upon them. The singers were instructed to chant the *Sh'ma Yisroel* (Hear O Israel) and lead the people in prayer. Profane songs of love and lust, the rabbis felt, were sufficient cause to destroy the world, but religious songs could save it. All instrumental music, even for religious purposes, was prohibited as a sign of national mourning. Abba Areka (Rav), at the beginning of the third century, stated that, "an ear which listens to (secular) music shall be torn out." A generation later, Rabba said, "Music in a house must bring the house to destruction." His colleague, Rav Joseph, expressed the opinion that, "if men sing and women respond, the result is licentiousness, but if women sing and men respond, the end is like a flame in hatcheled flax."

This attitude was not unique to the rabbis. At about the beginning of the Common Era, Greek art and culture degenerated to mere virtuosity, empty of any ideal. The music became a means by which to stimulate voluptuousness and was synonymous with obscenity. It was used primarily for carnal purposes at frivolous occasions. Christianity, like Judaism, fought the heathen music bitterly. Within a short time, no instrument was used in any Christian service. The strict order of the Church Fathers that only one instrument be employed, namely the human voice, is still observed in the Syriac, Jacobite, Nestorian and Greek churches. The synagogue, also, did not use any instrument in the service until 1810 when the organ was introduced in the first Reform Temple in Seesen, Germany. In the synagogue, unlike the Church, this prohibition also had a national motive, in that no musical instrument should be used until the Temple was restored and Levites would again conduct the musical service. Moreover, the playing of musical instruments on Sabbaths and festivals was regarded as a desecration.

The spiritual leaders' attitude regarding music could be found in several of their edicts. In Talmudic times, Rav Huna had zealously prohibited all secular music in the Babylonian Jewish community. It brought about a crisis in the market place for goods and services, for, without music, festivities and celebrations came to a halt. Becoming aware of the decree's danger, Rav Chisda cancelled the ruling. Nonetheless, restrictions were made as to which occasions were appropriate for instrumental music and to what degree they could be used. Thus, instruments were forbidden, not only on Sabbath and festivals but also on weekdays. They were, however, permitted at joyous occasions such as weddings. Even then, in an attempt to prevent over-indulgence in hilarity, a dish would be thrown and broken in front of the bride and groom, to remind them of the destruction of the Temple. In Talmudic times, when sages noticed an overabundance of gaiety at a wedding, they would suddenly break the most costly dishes, in order to shock the guests. This action is commemorated both prior to the traditional Jewish wedding ceremony and at its conclusion. After the *t'naim* (nuptial agreement) has been witnessed and read aloud, the mothers of the bride and groom break a dish. Also, as an act of remembrance, the groom shatters a glass with his foot just before the wedding ceremony ends. Both actions recall the breaking of dishes during those early times. Although the destruction of the Temple is the chief reason cited for refraining from music or any of its related arts, it was also the inherent nature and influential power of music that prompted the prohibition. The positions became polarized as evidenced by the following:

> When the Temple was destroyed it was decreed not to play any instrument of music or sing any songs, and all who sing songs are forbidden to be joyful. It is forbidden to let them be heard, because of the destruction, as written: 'The elders have ceased from the gate, the young men from their music,' (Lamentations 5:14) and song is forbidden to cross the lips unless it is in the praise of the Almighty. And above all, musical instruments are forbidden at feasts; they are prohibited even if there is no feast.
> (*Yosef Omets* by Rabbi Joseph Han-Nordlinge).

These words stress the motivating force behind the prohibition, mourning for the destruction of the Temple. The mourning must be real and perpetual, apparent even in the circumstances calling for joy such as that evoked by a bridal celebration. At all times one must share in Israel's sorrow, and never forget that the *Sh'chino* (Divine Presence) has been exiled from the Land of Israel. Music in all forms is identified with joy—the antithesis of grief. Joy and music are for the future in the time of total redemption as indicated in the passage, "Then was our mouth filled with laughter and our tongue with singing" (Ps. 226:2).

A steady stream of reports from the Middle Ages tells about Jewish minstrels and jugglers who, regardless of the rabbinic prohibitions against secular music, roamed the countryside performing before both Jews and Gentiles. Minstrelsy was an old vocation which had spread over the continent in the path of the Roman legions. Jews found and joined the universally open class of minstrels. This way of life continued for many Jews throughout the Middle Ages and beyond. Jewish communities themselves could not afford the luxury of offering a livelihood to this kind of artist. The minstrels sang, played musical instruments and memorized long epics which they recited. In addition, they danced, performed rope walking, and knife throwing. It was not uncommon to find a Jew as the court musician of a caliph, emir, Christian king, bishop or knight. The kings of Spain also held Jewish musicians in high esteem. They are repeatedly mentioned in the court accounts of the 14th-16th centuries. These Jewish musicians were welcome because they added flavor to the sometimes rather dull court atmosphere. They also appear in the company of troubadours and *trouvers*, like Suesskind of Trimberg (c. 1220), at the seat of the Bishop of Wuersberg. These Jewish singers mastered the international repertoire of their Gentile colleagues and, in addition, performed subject matter from the Bible and *Midrash*. The Jewish wandering minstrels served as intermediaries between the ghettos and their environment. They were also the bearers of an instrumental tradition, especially in the field of dance music. They brought to the Jewish quarter the outside music of the Gentile weddings and other happy occasions. It was not unusual for some of the dance melodies to find their way into synagogue song. It must be understood that the broad masses of people regulated musical taste by either giving or denying approval of certain melodies to the *chazan* (cantor). Conditions in the Jewish exile often did not allow for a delight in the refined art, and time and again Jews were thrown back to the level of poor people and to the kind of music enjoyed by that group of people. The rabbinic prohibition against all vocal and instrumental music outside the synagogue was never rescinded officially. In most Jewish communities, it was simply ignored.

A rejuvenated, ecstatic Jewish music was forced to wait for Hasidism, for joyousness and ecstasy were the cornerstones of this new folk movement. Hasidism proclaimed that joy and ecstasy can be achieved through song, and that one who is fearful can allay his fears with songs of joy. This coincides with the words of the Zohar: "For indeed we see that the Divinity is not present in a place of sadness but in a place in which there is joy. Where there is no joy, the Divinity does not rest."

THE MISINAI TUNES

Although the hasidic Rebbes and their adherents created a new body of melodies, two bodies of Jewish music remained constant. The chant style of the liturgical recitatives, the non-metrical music sung during religious services was a continuation of the chant style that preceded it in Jewish communities for centuries. A group of melodies known as the *Misinai* (from Mt. Sinai) *Tunes* were transmitted through generations and remained a permanent part of hasidic worship as it did in all other Ashkenazic communities. The *Ashkenazim* had created this genre of special tunes that had been "sanctified" and were known as *scarbove*. Several opinions as to the derivation of the word *scarbove* are extant. A.Z. Idelsohn, the renowned 20th century musicologist, believed *scarbove* to be a corruption of the Latin *sacra* (sacred). The music historian, Alfred Sendrey, expressed a dissenting view. He held *scarbove* to be derived from the Polish word *skarb* (treasure) and *scarbove* therefore means from the treasure house of the folk. The birthplace of these melodies was Southwestern Germany in the communities of Worms, Mayence, Speyer and the Rhineland. The name *Misinai* (from Mount Sinai) is an indication of the veneration with which these melodies were held. Perhaps the origin of the term can be found in the *Sefer Hasidim* in which the assertion is made that these songs were given to Moses at Mount Sinai. The melodies which belong to this category, and which are still adhered to in all Ashkenazic synagogues world wide, accompany liturgical texts from the High Holidays and the Festivals. They include, *Bar'chu* (from the evening service of the High Holidays), *Hamelech*, *Ovos*, *Olenu*, *Kol Nidre*, *V'hakohanim*, and *Kaddish* (recited before the High Holiday *Musaf* service, *N'ilah* service on Yom Kippur and for the *Tal* (Dew) and *Geshem* (Rain) prayers, recited during the *Passover* and *Sukot* festivals respectively). The most widely known Misinai tune is *Kol Nidre* which is chanted in all Ashkenazic synagogues world-wide on the eve of Yom Kippur, the Day of Atonement.

KOL NIDRE

Although the singing of *Kol Nidre* on Yom Kippur night precedes Hasidism, the melody and text of this prayer have been kept faithfully by the Rebbes and their followers A long-standing fable still exists in the minds of many with regard to *Kol Nidre*. There are those otherwise knowledgeable Jews who believe that both the text and the melody of this prayer emerged from the Spanish Inquisition. They assume that *Kol Nidre,* essentially a formula for self-absolution, was specifically designed to free those that had been forcibly converted from their imposed obligations. In this imaginary but vivid scene, the Marranos are seen gathering clandestinely in cellars or catacombs for the sacred service of the Day of Atonement. The Inquisitors are watching everywhere and the congregants are potential martyrs, for discovery means certain death. Despite the danger facing them, the Marranos recognize the holiness of the day and are determined to remain faithful to their ancestral tradition. This determination conquers the terror, which the possibility of discovery might inspire, and from their hearts bursts forth the melody of *Kol Nidre*. This imaginary picture has been so irresistible that a number of variations have been added. In an essay appearing in *Hashiloach*, Cantor Pinchas Minkovksy (1859-1924), a recognized author and musical scholar, wrote:

> And when we sing the Kol Nidre, it is not the dry legalistic formula of absolution, which stirs us. We are exalted by the memory of those crypto-Jews, hidden in cave and catacomb, wrapped in their tallithim, (prayer shawls) engaged in their prayer.

We see them again, fear upon their countenances, and in their hearts a pure devotion and an overwhelming desire to annul the vows and oaths which the agents of Torquemada had forced upon them.

Subsequently Minkovsky did correct himself, and, in an essay published in *Avodath Hakodesh* (Vienna), he approached the Spanish legend in an entirely different manner. He adopted the opposite extreme and tried to prove that the Ashkenazic *Kol Nidre* melody can claim no great antiquity because it displays tonal peculiarities that do not appear in music before the Renaissance.

In Volume V of his *Thesaurus of Oriental Melodies*, A.Z. Idelsohn notes that the *Sephardim*, the true heirs of the *Marranos*, sing *Kol Nidre* with a melody that differs entirely from that sung by *Ashkenazim*. Quite possibly, in reference to the essay in *Hashiloach*, he indulges in some sarcasm at the expense of Minkovsky.

The melody of the *Kol Nidre*, as it is sung by the Sephardim, has its roots in the melody with which the *Sephardim* intone the *S'lichot*; it has not the slightest relationship to the Ashkenazic *Kol Nidre* melody. And as for the fairy tale that this melody originated with the *Marranos* and was uttered by them in fear and in holiness as they gathered for the sacred service in their places of hiding, it is pure fantasy which inspired one of the cantors of Eastern Europe to promote this highly imaginative hypothesis.

The text of *Kol Nidre* was formally introduced by R. Yehudai Gaon (740 CE), but it seems that it had a different function at that time and most certainly a different melody. It was not repeated three times, nor did it have the present day preamble *B'y'shiva shel maala* (in the Academy on High). The practice of repeating the *Kol Nidre* was considered in a host of *Ashkenazic* rabbinic responsa. The most important, by *Maharil*, states that the *chazan* is "to extend the chant of the *Kol Nidre* until nightfall. He must chant the *Kol Nidre* three times, first in an undertone, then louder during the first repetition and even louder for the third, for then we shall hearken with awe and trembling." Nowhere does the *Maharil* refer to any specific tune for the text but speaks only of "long drawn out melodies."

The first version of the melody appeared in a collection of liturgical synagogue chants published in 1785 by Ahron Beer, a cantor in Berlin. Although his transcription contains most of the familiar elements, the melody continued to change. One hundred years later, the renowned Louis Lewandowski transcribed the melody as it appears in this volume. Many variants appear and continue to appear. A number of musicians arranged *Kol Nidre* for cantor and both male and mixed choir as well as organ. The melody, although with many variations brought on by several hundred years of oral transmission, is sung in all Ashkenazic synagogues, including Conservative, Reconstructionist, Reform as well as Orthodox and Hasidic synagogues.

In 1826, Ludwig von Beethoven was commissioned by the Jewish community in Vienna to compose a cantata for the dedication of their new Temple. Although the composer considered this idea for a while, he later declined. The task was accomplished by his pupil, the composer Seyfried. It may very well be that, while Beethoven was considering this commission, he began to look into Jewish thematic material, and that *Kol Nidre* was brought to his attention. We find the theme of *Kol Nidre* woven throughout Beethoven's C#minor string quartet, opus 131, composed during that period.

Max Bruch, a nineteenth century composer, wrote a *Kol Nidre* for cello and orchestra which has become a well known show piece for virtuoso cellists. Although the composition opens with recognizable elements of the chant, it then digresses into lyric romantic passages which have almost no relationship to the original. Far less frequently performed, but much closer to the melody and spirit of the chant, is the *Kol Nidre* by the great twentieth century composer, Arnold Schoenberg. Written in 1938 for chorus, orchestra and "speaker," it had its premiere in 1958, seven years after the death of the composer.

Schoenberg's *Kol Nidre* has an interesting history. Although born a Jew, the composer had converted to Christianity in his youth. Subsequently he shunned all religious affiliation. The Nazis drove him, along with many other great artists, to find refuge in the United States. He settled in Los Angeles where he met Rabbi Jacob Sonderling, a mystical and poetic soul. The rabbi was able to stir Schoenberg's Jewish feelings to such a degree that the composer resolved to return formally to Judaism. His "act of contrition"– symbolic of his reconversion—was this *Kol Nidre.*

"In reality, for those who understand what they hear, a song tells more than a story.

—Rabbi Shneur Zalman of Liadi

KOL NIDRE

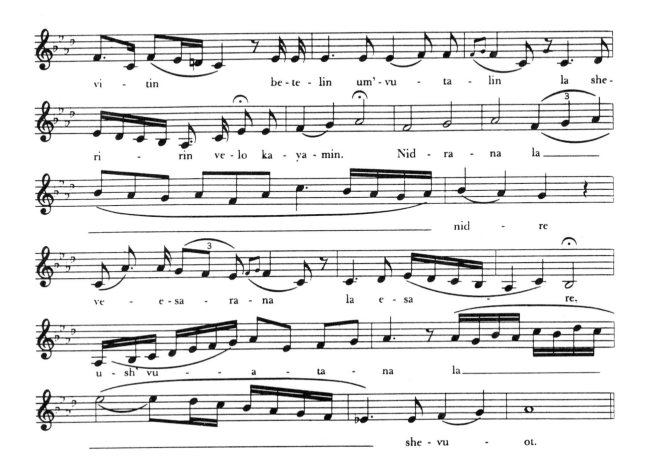

vi - tin be - te - lin um' - vu - ta - lin la she -
ri - rin ve - lo ka - ya - min. Nid - ra - na la _____
nid - re
ve - e - sa - ra - na la e - sa - re,
u - sh' vu - a - ta - na la _____
she - vu - ot.

כָּל נִדְרֵי · וֶאֱסָרֵי · וַחֲרָמֵי · וְקוֹנָמֵי · וְכִנּוּיֵי · וְקִנּוּסֵי ·
וּשְׁבוּעוֹת · דִּנְדַרְנָא · וּדְאִשְׁתַּבַּעְנָא · וּדְאַחֲרִימְנָא ·
וְדַאֲסַרְנָא עַל נַפְשָׁתָנָא · מִיּוֹם כִּפֻּרִים זֶה עַד יוֹם כִּפֻּרִים
הַבָּא עָלֵינוּ לְטוֹבָה · כֻּלְּהוֹן אִחֲרַטְנָא בְהוֹן · כֻּלְּהוֹן יְהוֹן
שָׁרָן · שְׁבִיקִין · שְׁבִיתִין · בְּטֵלִין וּמְבֻטָּלִין · לָא שְׁרִירִין
וְלָא קַיָּמִין: נִדְרָנָא לָא נִדְרֵי · וֶאֱסָרָנָא לָא אֱסָרֵי ·
וּשְׁבוּעָתָנָא לָא שְׁבוּעוֹת:

All vows, bonds, promises, obligations and oaths [to God] which we have vowed, sworn and bound ourselves: from this Day of Atonement until the next Day of Atonement, may it come to us for good: all these we repent. They shall be absolved, released, annulled, made void, and to no effect: they shall not be binding nor shall they have any power. Our vows [to God] shall not be vows: our bonds shall not be bonds: and our oaths shall not be oaths.

HASIDIC MUSIC-AN OVERVIEW

Hasidic song is a living testament, unique in the folk music of the world. It illuminates the people among whom it took root, and who, through every condition of adversity and joy, have nourished and preserved it to the present moment, and prepared it for a secure posterity. It bears eloquent witness to the continuity of Jewish history, to the immovable conviction that the sacred encompasses all of life, and to the faith of the believer in the continuing presence and strength of God's love.

It is an endless, deep song. We must first listen to it carefully. But we must also understand its place in Jewish history, its structure as music, the specific uses to which it has been put by the Jewish community, past and present, and its condition and influence in our time. We begin, as the music itself does, with tradition.

The origin of hasidic music may be traced to the *Ari,* Rabbi Isaac Luria (1534-1572), and to the Kabbalist movement. The Kabbalists in Palestine made singing their duty and considered it a condition of inspiration and devotion. Melody stood at the cradle of Kabbalah and surrounded it with the mystic yearnings that have touched the hearts of its followers to this day. The hasidic movement, heir to the Kabbalists, assigned to music a position of primary importance.

It is true that following the destruction of the Temple and during hundreds of years of Jewish life in the Diaspora, music was kept at a minimum. "How can I sing the song of the Lord in a strange land?" asked the Psalmist (Psalm 137). Nevertheless, the development of Jewish music never ceased. Music remained the duty of the heart and found expression in small ways—the study *nigun* (tune) associated with the learning of the Talmud, the synagogue chant, and the singing at weddings and other festive occasions. This music, however, was limited since a people under the constant yoke of oppression finds little occasion to express itself in song.

According to the rabbis of Eastern Europe, a *nigun* is created only to bring joy and pleasure. It followed that music, which brought pleasure to its performers and listeners, was not in keeping with the generally sad state of the Jews in the Diaspora. Along the way, the rabbis permitted one *nigun* to be sung on the Sabbath. But even those *nigunim* which were allowed were generally of a sad nature and were adapted to such texts as "I will set Jerusalem above my chiefest joy." (Psalm 137)

The Baal Shem Tov (1700-1760), founder of the Hasidic movement, arrived on the East European scene at a time when Jewish morale was extremely low. The long-awaited and hoped for Messiah, in the person of Shabtai Zvi, had proven false, and the Jews had been left totally disheartened. They took to fasting on Mondays and Thursdays; many wore ashes on their foreheads and sackcloth on their shoulders. A divided Jewish community added to this feeling of moroseness. Jews were placed in a quasi caste system, with the Torah scholars heading the list, and the unlearned individuals at the bottom. The Baal Shem Tov realized that this system, combined with the general sadness of the Jewish community, made Judaism unappealing. It was necessary to develop a system with a framework within which the lowly unlearned as well as the scholar could feel assured of worth and dignity. The movement that he founded, a movement appealing to the masses, was his answer.

The system of prayers, observance of *mitzvos* (commandments) and *ma'asim tovim* (good deeds) had, by his time, become arid and lackluster. The return to a meaningful and vibrant Judaism, the Baal Shem Tov felt, must contain *simcho* (joy) an ingredient too long denied it. Joy became a cornerstone of Hasidism. Had not the Psalmist said, "Serve the Lord with joy—come before Him with singing"? (Psalm 100). The concept of *simcho* was not a new idea, but rather a return to the past. *Simcho* had always been considered a fundamental characteristic of the Jewish people. The commandment, "And you shall rejoice in your festivals and you shall be altogether joyful," is found in the Bible (Deuteronomy 16:14). Of course, the biblical *simcho* aims for the elevation of the body and soul in the service of God, and is not unrestrained joy for its own sake. Joy without this elevation is not entitled to the term *simcho*. It is interesting to note the number of synonyms for *simcho* which are found in the Hebrew language. *Gilo, soson, alitso, alizo, tsohol, chedvo*, and *ditso* all express various degrees of joy.

The Baal Shem Tov insisted that a revitalized Judaism must do away with the self-imposed custom of fasting and the denial of worldly things. He believed that a lively and joyous manner was more acceptable to God than asceticism; melancholy and morbidity were, to him, sinful. "Only through *simcho* can we attain communion with God," he said. The Baal Shem Tov also realized that, when one is happy, he views life through a bright and clear looking glass. He therefore returned the joy of living and the vision of a new world—a people of *soson v'simcho, ahavo v'achavo* —to Judaism.

The Baal Shem Tov proclaimed that the *Shchino* (Divine Presence) rests upon a person only when he is happy, not when he is sad, and even if one has committed a transgression, he should not be morose. He should rather feel complete remorse for his transgression and immediately return to joyful communion with the Lord, the Creator. The ecstasy of melody and joy are the keys with which Hasidism strives to unlock the gates of heaven. They are, so to speak, the ladder to the throne of God. The Baal Shem Tov proclaimed,

Through the unfathomable depths of space wander countless stars, luminous thoughts of God-blessed instruments on which the Creator plays. They are all happy—for God desires a happy world.

Joy is the creed of the hasid. This is his religion. He shows his faith primarily through joy. Music, the natural concomitant of joy, fills the head with a holy ecstasy of unearthly happiness. The Baal Shem Tov preached that the simple man, imbued with native faith and able to pray fervently and wholeheartedly with a sense of joy in his heart, was nearer and dearer to God than the learned but joyless formalist who spent his whole life studying the Talmud. The essence of faith, he taught, lies in the emotions, not in the intellect. The more profound the emotions, the nearer man is to God.

The elevation of song to an exalted pinnacle was nothing radically new. Hasidic song is, in essence, a return to the origin, and a renewal of ties that had been temporarily broken. The Besht (contraction of Baal Shem Tov), while he founded a new movement, in no way minimized or discarded any of the spiritual foundations which had become part of Judaism during its early development. In addition to these foundations, Hasidism recognized the power of the *nigun* and knew that melody had the ability to purify and bind together the soul and to elevate it to great heights. This also was not a new concept, for the *Kabbalists* had already stated, "Access to certain temples can be achieved only through song" (Zohar, Genesis).

It is strange to note that in the sayings attributed to the Baal Shem Tov we do not find many references to his belief in or attachment to music. However, from the many legends, and writings of his followers, we learn that song was a natural part of the Besht's body and soul. The stories regarding his singing ability and affinity for song are countless. We find that he spent much time among the shepherds in the fields and absorbed many of their melodies which he regarded as possessing a *nitsots shel k'dusha* (a spark of holiness).

In the hasidic writings, we do find the statement that, "prayer performed with joy is more acceptable to God than prayer which is accompanied by sadness and tears." The Beshtian School, faithful to this concept of song, was characterized primarily by happy sounding and rhythmic melodies. The strains of shepherd melodies evident in the Beshtian music in no way harmed the sanctity of the melody. The essence of a *nigun*, according to Hasidism, is the sound, and, if the sound is derived from impure sources, there is a duty to elevate, purify, and sanctify it until it is worthy of the responsibility for which it was created. Like the zealous Christians of the Middle Ages, some of the hasidic leaders considered it a holy duty to use secular tunes for sacred purposes. Many leaders felt that this was a greater accomplishment than creating an original melody.

Those who opposed Hasidism, and many music scholars who made little effort to understand the soul of hasidic music, never failed to emphasize that foreign elements could be found within its melodies. It is important to note, however, that the borrowed motifs never remained as they had originally been; rather, they were changed and reshaped into a new form by the hasidim. Thus, a new melody evolved into the hasidic *nigun*.

Most Rebbes lived in residences, which were called "courts" by their followers. Each major dynasty had its own court. The size and character of each court varied in accordance with the number of adherents and the degree of their wealth, since the courts were supported solely by gifts from the hasidim. Devotees of a Rebbe would come as pilgrims to these courts, often traveling great distances by foot or primitive transportation, leaving home and family to spend the Festivals or the High Holidays with the Rebbe. Often, specific Sabbaths were set aside as gatherings in a given Rebbe's court. In the presence of the Rebbe, and in the midst of joyous fellowship and camaraderie, the hasid would forget his daily worries and anxieties. At the conclusion of his stay, he would return home, spiritually revitalized and assured that he could transcend his lot.

It was on the Sabbath and festivals, during the services and at the *tish* (the communal meals with the Rebbe), that new melodies were introduced and older ones brought back. Often the Rebbe himself sang the new *nigunim*; at other times, they were taught to the hasidim by the Rebbe's son or by the *gabbai* (assistant to the Rebbe). Having sung these tunes repeatedly throughout the Sabbath or Festival, the hasidim were able to introduce them to family, friends and neighbors upon their return home. Thus, without musical transcriptions or the possibility of recording, a large body of song was transmitted orally throughout Europe and served as a repertoire for far-flung hasidic groups.

Most of the original hasidic melodies were composed by the Rebbes themselves. Rabbi Levi Yitschok of Berditchev (1740-1810) was a prolific composer and introduced liturgical recitative into the body of hasidic song (See *A Dudele* page 154). The famous *Alter Rebbe's Nigun* (See page 95), composed by Rabbi Shneur Zalman of Liadi (1747-1813), is still sung today.

Rabbi Nachman of Bratslav (1772-1810) was perhaps the greatest poet of the hasidic movement. Like his grandfather, the *Besht*, before him, Rabbi Nachman spent much time outdoors in the natural surroundings of his town, Mezhiboz, when he was a child. Nature opened a new world for him, and he began to understand that which many others before him did not or could not. Just as the harp of King David played by itself when the north wind touched its strings, so did Rabbi Nachman's heart fill with music when he beheld the forests, hills, brooks, and other aspects of nature.

He loved music with a consuming passion and earnestness, and felt the presence of melody in every aspect of nature. Flowers, grass, trees, the sun and moon, even the human body, were to him brimming over with song. "Every science," he said, "every religion, every philosophy has its own pattern of song. The higher the religion or science the more exalted its music." It was Rabbi Nachman who, loving *neginah* with all his might and soul, placed it on its loftiest height. Since the time of the *Zohar*, when the virtues of the *nigun* were lauded, no one had spoken with such intensity about music as did Rabbi Nachman. The *nigun* became the foundation for his lectures and sermons. The amount of his *Torah* discourse dedicated to song reached phenomenal heights; in this respect, none of the rabbinic writings can compare with his. Sadly, however, the man who placed such emphasis on the power and importance of *neginah* did not create compositions himself; rather, he commissioned composers of greater or lesser merit to compose *nigunim*. The songs of the Bratslav Hasidim are less familiar than those of other dynasties, but many of them became part of the body of Lubavitch and Karliner melodies.

The possession of a pleasing voice and the ability to compose a *nigun* were great assets to a hasidic leader. Like Rabbi Nachman, many Rebbes did not possess the ability to create music. This God-given gift was denied them. The first Rebbe and founder of the Ger dynasty regretfully observed to his hasidim, "Were I blessed with a sweet and beautiful voice, I could sing for you new hymns every day, for with the daily rejuvenation of the world, new songs are being created." Echoing a similar thought, Rabbi Pinchos of Koretz proclaimed, "If I were a singer, I would accept upon myself the duty of traveling from city to city in order to lead prayers in the various congregations. "

When Rebbes found their vocal or creative skills to be lacking, they appointed or "hired" singers, usually from among their hasidim. It was the duty of these hasidim to study the mood, emotions, and thoughts of the Rebbe and to express them through song. However, the singer's choices were limited to new songs that he created or existing songs of his court; were he to intone melodies belonging to another court, he would be dismissed. If an original tune was accepted by the Rebbe, the court-created melody was usually credited to the composer's Rebbe.

Some leaders were opposed to old tunes from "yesterday." The Tsadik of Kuzmir (1806-1856) proclaimed that a Sabbath without a new *nigun* was not truly a Sabbath. Following the Rebbe's inspiration, the hasidim would invent new meditations and set them to tunes. The lyrics for many of these new tunes are often a mixture of Hebrew and Yiddish. The *nigunim* of Rabbi Levi Yitschok of Berditchev are typical of this genre, (See *A Dudele* page 154). He knew that Yiddish was the language understood by the common masses; although Hebrew was part of the daily services, the ordinary Jew often found it difficult to understand fully.

The majority of the early hasidic songs were wordless. It is difficult to ascertain if the song without words was known to Judaism before the advent of Hasidism. We do know, however, that, even before Hasidism, it was common practice for many cantors to employ sections of melody alone, without benefit of text. This was called a *Shtel* and served as an introduction to a liturgical composition. The *Shtel*, however, can in no way be compared to the wordless songs of the hasidim. There are, to be sure, modern songs that have wordless interludes, and many classic art songs have such moments. In addition, this type of singing can be found among some African groups and, of course, in nursery songs for children. Among the hasidim, a song without words functions as a mantra. Songs without words, but full of religious ecstasy, were created on the premise that a song without words is much better than one with words. King David had stated, "Words alone cannot relate the greatness of God." "Melody is the outpouring of the soul," said the first Lubavitcher Rebbe, Rabbi Shneur Zalman of Liadi, "Words interrupt the stream of emotions." A melody with text, according to him, is limited in time, for, with the conclusion of the words, the melody also ends. A tune without words, however, can be repeated endlessly.

In order to fill the void created by the absence of text, it is possible to hum a melody. It is difficult, however, to hum a melody for an extended period, especially if it is a rhythmical *rikud* (dance) melody. In order to facilitate the singing of such melodies, hasidim invented a group of vocalized syllables. Syllables such as *bim bam*, *yadi-dadi*, *aha aha*, *ya-ma-ma-ma*, *na-na-na-na* etc., had no specific order or pattern; the singer was at liberty to vocalize in response to the mood of the music. A song of sad nature would often use *oy vey*, which has been the traditional Jewish cry of anguish. Various hasidic groups used specific vocalized syllables, which became a stylistic hallmark of their singing. Accordingly, it often was easy for an ethnomusicologist to pinpoint the area and dynastic origin of a melody, based on the syllables employed. The *Misnagdim* (opponents of Hasidism) and other non-devotees of Hasidism found much to parody in the use of such vocalized sounds, and they wrote numerous satirical songs (see Parodies) utilizing hasidic syllables in order to poke fun at a Rebbe, his hasidim and their songs.

It is worth noting that the musical compositions of the first hasidim were not distinguished by their length. By and large, they were short and were comprised of only a few sections. Lubavitch hasidim expanded on this by adding several sections to the typical *nigun*. Hasidim in Poland went even further in lengthening the *nigun*. This style was taken over by hasidim in Galicia and some *nigunim* became so lengthy that they were titled "operas." The best of these can be found among the lengthy *operas* of the Modzitz dynasty (see page 166). In the hasidic synagogues of Alexander and Ger, the *Shovuos* poem *Akdomus* was usually sung to lengthy *nigunim*.

One must bear in mind that the music of the hasidim is strictly an oral tradition. With very few exceptions, the *nigunim* were transmitted from memory. For various reasons, hasidic leaders issued prohibitions against committing *nigunim* to paper in musical form. They felt that once written down, these melodies would enter the public domain and might be used in a manner which might corrupt their initial intent. In addition, it was felt that even sophisticated musical notation could not adequately express the soul and pathos evoked in the singing of these songs. In fact, it is known that a number of songs did find their way into print and were used by individuals and institutions not dedicated to Jewish worship.

Melodies created during the early years of the Hasidic Movement fall within three distinct categories: the *tish nigun*, *dvekus* and *rikud*. The *tish nigun* is a long, slow, meditative melody sung at the Rebbe's table, usually not by him but by his son or one of the hasidim. It has several parts, often in varying moods, with a refrain towards the end. Between sections, there may be a *wolloch* (pastoral melody from Wallachia) which rises coloratura-like, simulating a shepherd playing his flute. The *dvekus* (union, cleaving to God), or Torah melody, is a slow, introspective, soul stirring song, usually lengthy and sung with deep feeling. Hasidim often sang this type of song when they were absorbed at the study desk or just before the Rebbe began his Torah discourse. The *rikud* (dance tune) was usually in a three part ABCB form, that is to say, a three-section song with the second section repeated. Many of these songs were in the major scale, and even those in the minor mode had a happy lilt to them. Many of these dance tunes would be sung for as long as half an hour, until the dancers were spent or a new melody was introduced. The *rikud* was also sung at the *tish* and in the synagogue service as a *nigun* set to a liturgical text.

As hasidic music developed, several other styles became popular. Hasidim encountered the military on parade and heard, and absorbed various march tunes. Although such militaristic songs were quite foreign to the entire spirit of Judaism at the time, many liturgical texts from the Sabbath and Festival prayers were set to these march rhythms. Similarly, the hasidim were attracted to the waltz, which was permeating European society of the 19th and early 20th centuries. Hasidic composers, in particular the Modzitzer Rebbes, found the 3/4 time rhythm intriguing. Rabbi Saul, the second Rebbe of Modzitz, would compose at least one new waltz for the *Hallel* text *B'tses Yisroel* each year. Modern day Jewish musicians and writers knew little of the nature of hasidim and their attraction to certain types of melodies and rhythms. The well-known conductor, composer and music critic, Sholem Secunda, in reviewing my collections, *Songs of the Hasidim Vols. 1 & 2*, published in the early 1970s, wrote that he was favorably impressed with the effort and research that went into these collections. He did, however, take the editor to task. "For all of his fine scholarship, Mr. Pasternak has made a grievous error. He has included twenty waltz melodies set to liturgical texts," (most of which were compositions of the Rebbes of Modzitz). "Frankly I cannot visualize a Rebbe waltzing with his hasidim on a dance floor." Secunda failed to understand that just as the hasidic march melodies were not meant for marching, so were the waltz melodies not meant for dancing. If there were appealing musical styles that were being heard or played in the secular Polish or Russian culture, hasidim felt they should adopt and adapt them to religious texts for use in worship and other religious activities.

Rather unique in the body of hasidic song are the recitatives of Rabbi

Levi Yitzchok of Berditchev. Two of the most famous are *A Dudele* (see page 154), and *A Din Toire Mit Gott* (See page 156). Both compositions set to Yiddish texts, have remained in the repertoire of cantors and singers and are among the most often performed hasidic songs. Explaining the use of Yiddish vernacular in prayers, Reb Nachman of Bratslav (1772-1810), a grandson of the Baal Shem Tov, said: "Seclusion is the highest stage in which man can attain inspiration, where he can pour out his heart to God in a free and intimate way, and in the language familiar to him, in his native tongue. In our country this is Yiddish, for Hebrew is little known to the average man, and consequently it is difficult for him to express himself in it fluently. Therefore, whenever Hebrew is used as a medium of prayer, the ears do not hear what the mouth utters." Hasidim reported that, "Reb Levi Yitzchok at first sang with deep humility, like one weeping for mercy from the bottom of his heart...then a great joy and ecstasy almost to fainting...It is impossible to describe how deeply stirred his disciples were. Everyone felt that the tune had brought them into a higher, unknown world."

Most hasidic Rebbes and their musically adept adherents created or appropriated melodies for use within their own group. Those *nigunim* that became popular often entered the repertoire of other hasidic courts, especially the smaller ones. Among the musically acknowledged groups were Belz, Bobov, Vishnitz, and Karlin /Stolin. In a long-standing tradition, a major hasidic dynasty, Ger, maintained a *Kapelye* (male choral group) which sang at High Holidays and Sabbath during the year. A legacy of popular melodies, many in the style of peasant dances composed by Rabbi Yankel Talmud, made up a large portion of the Ger repertoire. In keeping with Ger philosophy, new nigunim were created annually by the official court composers. Many of Talmud's tunes were transcribed and appear in *Malchin L'bes Gur* (Composer to the Court of Ger) published in 1963. It was in this book, as well as in advertisements in England and newspapers on the European Continent, that Rabbi Talmud asked for help with regard to his own compositions. "Rabbi

Yaacov Talmud, the hasidic composer, is touring Britain and the Continent on a very unusual quest. He is searching for people who can remember the tunes he composed before leaving Poland for Israel in 1933, as he wants to have a complete collection. In those days Rabbi Talmud did not write down his compositions." Because of these ads, he did meet several people who recalled his songs for him. Several of them subsequently appeared on a series of recordings of Ger melodies and are still popular among many hasidic groups.

"How do you pray to the Lord? Is it possible to pray to the Lord with words alone? Come, I will show you a new way to the Lord—not with words or sayings, but with song. We will sing, and the Lord on high will understand us. "

—Rabbi Nachman of Bratslav

MUSIC OF MODZITZ

Nowhere within Hasidism did music assume a greater role than in the dynasty of Modzitz. Music and Modzitz became synonymous. In his book, *Lahasidim Mizmor* (Jerusalem 1955), the eminent authority on the music of the hasidim, M.S. Geshuri, compares the city of Modzitz, and its influence on the musical life of Eastern European Jewry, to Bayreuth and its affect on the devotees of Richard Wagner. The Modzitzer dynasty was founded by Rabbi Yisroel Taub (b. 1848, Ratcoinz, Poland; d. 1920, Warsaw, Poland). In 1888, upon the death of his father, Rabbi Samuel Eliyahu of Zvolyn, Rabbi Yisroel assumed the leadership of Kuzmir-Zvolyn Hasidim. In 1891, he settled in Modzitz and resided there until the outbreak of World War I in 1914, when he fled to Warsaw. Rabbi Israel composed more than two hundred *nigunim*. One of his most famous tunes, the *Heimloz Nigun* (the "Song of the Homeless"), was set to the text of Psalm 123, and became a Jewish classic. In it, the Rebbe gives musical expression to the feelings of a Jew torn from his home due to war.

Rabbi Yisroel's most famous *nigun* is the lengthy *Ezk'ro Hagodol* (the Great *Ezk'ro*). Chassidic legend relates the following with regard to its creation. In 1913, at the age of sixty-three, Rabbi Israel fell ill and was forced to travel to Berlin for medical treatment. His doctors felt that his life could be saved only by the amputation of a leg. While awaiting surgery, the Rebbe could look out the window next to his bed and see the surrounding area of Berlin. The architecture and color of the buildings were similar to Jerusalem and the poem *Ez'kro Elohim,* written about the holy city and recited during the closing service on *Yom Kippur* came to his mind. The Rebbe agreed to the operation but with the provision that no form of anesthesia be used. During the removal of the leg, he composed this *nigun*. The doctors were amazed at the serenity of their patient. "In the room next to you," the surgeon, Professor James Adolph

Israel, told him, "I have a patient who is a cabinet minister. He constantly wails and moans, and I said to him, 'You ought to be ashamed of yourself. I have an old rabbi next door, and whenever he is in pain he sings.'" Rabbi Israel replied, "I, too, moaned and wailed, but my pain turned into song." Subsequently he developed this melody into an extended composition with thirty-six motifs, considered by many to be the masterpiece of hasidic song. *Ezk'ro Elohim* takes approximately one half hour to sing. It can be heard each year on the Rebbe's *yahrzeit* (anniversary of death) in Modzitzer synagogues in Israel and the United States. The *nigun* was transcribed by M.S. Geshuri, and can be found in his book, *Bais Kuzmir* (Jerusalem, Israel).

Modzitzer philosophy explains the emphasis on music and musical creativity. Rabbi Yisroel pointed to the word *habocher* which appears in two blessings, one preceding the *Barchu* prayer of the *Shacharit* service, and the other recited immediately before the reading of the *Haftorah*. In the first instance, the text reads *habocher b'shire zimro* (Blessed are You O Lord Our God who is pleased with songs and hymns), while the second blessing contains the words *habocher batorah* (Blessed are You O Lord our God who has chosen the Torah). These two *habocher*, Torah and melody, became the foundation of the Modzitzer dynasty and its greatest contribution to hasidic life.

The music of the Modzitzer Rebbes became well known and beloved in almost every Polish city and hamlet in which Jews lived. The Modzitzer Rebbes, unlike many of their predecessors, did not formulate new ideas or philosophies within Hasidism. They did, however, create a true spiritual center— a center built primarily on music. Although small in comparison to such grand courts as Bobov, Ger, Lubavitch, Sanz, Belz, Vishnitz and others, Modzitz became a household word throughout the Jewish pale.

Rabbi Yisroel's love for music also found expression in several of his published *mamorim* (sayings). A remarkable thought, based on music, is found in his book, *Divre Yisroel*. The Modzitzer Rebbe compares man's ascent on the ladder of life to a musical scale. Just as the eighth tone of the scale is a repetition of the root tone one octave higher, so, too, he says, is man's climb throughout life. Although he progresses ever higher, becoming complacent in his achievement, he must be aware that ultimately he must return to the root, the bottom rung.

In 1944, towards the end of World War II, the Modzitzer Rebbe, Rabbi Saul Taub, came to my hometown, Toronto, Canada. He had been visiting this Jewish community annually for a number of years, and hasidim and music lovers eagerly looked forward to these annual visits. He spent several weeks in the city and directed the *tish* each Friday night, *Shabbat* afternoon and at the *Melave Malka* (post Sabbath celebratory meal). He offered original Torah discourses and a wealth of old, well-known Modzitz melodies as well as newly created *nigunim*. The new melodies, especially, became the musical treasure house for the coming year. They were introduced in many synagogues and were sung during the services on Sabbath and festivals as well as for *z'mirot* (Sabbath songs sung in the home).

Rabbi Saul composed his melodies in a number of styles— *wolloch* (pastoral type melody), *rikud* (rhythmical dance melody), waltz and march   At a Third Meal one Sabbath afternoon when I was nine years old, I had the great privilege of sitting with my father very close to the Rebbe. Sitting close was very important to me because I was intrigued by the percussive accompaniment of the Rebbe's hands while he sang a *nigun*. He drummed continuously as he sang. On this occasion, he introduced a regal march tune. When he finished, one of the congregants shouted at the Rebbe and said, "Rebbe I don't understand! Jews are being burned in the crematoria. We do not have a country of our own, nor do we possess a flag. We do not have an army, tanks or an air force. Why are you busy creating marches, and for whom?" The Rebbe smiled softly. "You are right," he said, "we do not have all that is necessary for nationhood. However, will it not be a shame, when we do have our own land, our own soldiers, and our own flag, and we can only borrow marches from the great band masters of the world?" To the lasting tribute of the Modzitzer Rebbe, a number of marches which he composed when no one more than dreamed of a Jewish State, found their way into the band repertoire of modern Israel and are played alongside those of the world band- masters. Most hasidic melodies are brief snatches of song. The Modzitzer Rebbes were among the few hasidic composers who created sustained, developed works. Because these large pieces are revered as supreme expressions of devotion in hasidic music, they are referred to as "operas" in the sense of masterpieces. Rabbi Saul was the composer of five " operas." The first, written in 1920, was designed to carry both singers and listeners through various stages of meditation and spiritual awakening until they reach the final ecstasy of joyous communion

From a musical standpoint, Modzitzer *nigunim* are more interesting both in melody and structure than those of other hasidic courts. This is probably due to the fact that the Rebbes of Modzitz were blessed with innate musicianship although they were not trained formally in music. Rabbi Saul even thought in terms of orchestral coloration; and, in reference to a melody he had just sung, was once heard to say, "This section could use a trumpet and the other section some strings." Although many *nigunim* were created and remained popular among hasidic groups such as Bobov, Ger, Vishnitz, Karlin, Breslov etc., it is the Modzitzer *nigun* which became the paradigm for all hasidic *nigunim*. Their musical creations were held in such awe that even knowledgeable writers fell prey to unsubstantiated information. Isaschar Fater, a noted Jewish music historian, writing in his book, *Jewish Music in Poland Between the Two World Wars*, claims that Rabbi Israel "taught himself notes from a book, *M'natse'ach Binginot — Gezang Meister* (by Zvi Nison Golombek). "The Rebbe's son, Rabbi Saul," Fater writes, "was a proficient reader and had, with great diligence, studied music theory."

The Modzitzer Rebbes were the most prolific of all hasidic composers. (Rabbi Israel's output-approximately two hundred *nigunim*; Rabbi Saul-approximately seven hundred (only about half of which survive); Rabbi Samuel Eliyah-approximately 400.) Paying tribute to his father, Rabbi Israel, Rabbi Saul said: "Before my father, hasidic music was mere folksong. He raised it to the level of art." The wide popularity of Modzitzer music is due primarily to a series of recordings initiated by Ben Zion Shenker. At age 15, Shenker became an ardent admirer of Rabbi Saul and served as his musical secretary, transcribing many of the Rebbe's compositions during the years 1940-1947. *Melave Malke Melodies*, the first recording of hasidic music, issued in 1956, featured Shenker as soloist accompanied by a chorus of hasidic singers. This recording was followed two years later by *Sholosh R'golim* (Three Festivals). The *Modzitzer Favorites* series, issued in the early 1960's, spread the music of Modzitz to Jewish communities all over the world.

"I cannot sit at the Sabbath table without a new song. There is no festive Sabbath without a new song."

—Tsadik of Kuzmir

RIKUD
CD TRACK NO. 1

In the *Rikud* (dance), hasidim find physical expression of their fervent and ardent faith. Moved by flaming enthusiasm, hasidim dance as the ultimate expression of their union with the Divine. The third Modzitzer Rebbe, Rabbi Samuel Elijah, composed both of these dance melodies, the first is often sung with the text of Shir Hama'alos (Psalm 126).

RIKUD No. 2

EN KITZVO
CD TRACK No. 3

March

Modzitz

Én kitz -vo -lish - no - se - cho v' - én kétz l' - o -
rech yo - me - cho v'-én l'-sha-ér mar-k'-vos k'-vo-de - cho

v'-én l'-fo-résh é-lum sh'-me-cho
ba-a-vur k'-vod shim-cho
shi-m'-cho no-e l'-cho

v'-a-to no-e lish-me-cho ush-mé-nu
ha-na-a-rotz ha-na-a-rotz v'-ha-nik-dosh k'-sod si-ach

ko-ro-so bish-me-cho ush-mé-nu ko-ro-so
sa-r'-fe ko-desh ha-mak-di-shim shim-cho ba-ko-desh

Fine

ko-ro-so bish-me-cho bim bom bim
do-ré ma-lo im do-ré ma-to ke-ser

a-sé l'-ma-an sh'-me-cho v'-ka-
(bim bom) (bim bom)

86

desh es shim-cho al mak-di - shé sn' - me-cho sh' - me-cho

En kits-vo lish-no-se-cho
V'-en ketz l'-o-rech yo-me-cho
V'-en l'-sha-er mar-k'-vos k'-vo-de-cho
V'-en l'-fo-resh i-lum sh'-me-cho
Shim-cho no-e loch v'-a-to no-e lish-me-cho
V'-ka-desh es shim-cho al mak-di-she sh'-me-cho
Ba-a-vur k'-vod shim-cho
Ha-na-a-rots v'-ha-nik-dosh
K'-sod si-ach sar-fe ko-desh
Ha-mak-di-shim shim-cho ba-ko-desh
Do-re ma-lo
Im do-re ma-to, keser

אֵין קִצְבָה לִשְׁנוֹתֶיךָ
וְאֵין קֵץ לְאֹרֶךְ יָמֶיךָ.
וְאֵין לְשַׁעֵר מַרְכְּבוֹת כְּבוֹדֶךָ
וְאֵין לְפָרֵשׁ עִילוּם שְׁמֶךָ
שִׁמְךָ נָאֶה לְךָ וְאַתָּה נָאֶה לִשְׁמֶךָ
וּשְׁמֵנוּ קָרָאתָ בִּשְׁמֶךָ
עֲשֵׂה לְמַעַן שְׁמֶךָ
וְקַדֵּשׁ אֶת שִׁמְךָ עַל מַקְדִּישֵׁי שְׁמֶךָ
בַּעֲבוּר כְּבוֹד שְׁמֶךָ
הַנַּעֲרָץ וְהַנִּקְדָּשׁ
כְּסוֹד שִׂיחַ שַׂרְפֵי קֹדֶשׁ
הַמַּקְדִּישִׁים שְׁמֶךָ בַּקּוֹדֶשׁ
דָּרֵי מַעְלָה
עִם דָּרֵי מַטָּה, כֶּתֶר.

The years have no measure nor have Your days any end. None can conceive the chariots of Your glory, nor fathom the mystery of Your name. Your name befits You and You are according to Your name, and you have linked our name with Your own. O do it for the sake of Your name and sanctify Your name through them that call it holy; for Your glorious name's sake, which is revered and sanctified by the mystic utterance of the holy Seraphim who hallow it in the sanctuary, they that dwell in the heavens uniting those who dwell on earth.

This march is set to the text from the High Holiday *Musaf* service following the well-known *Un'sane Tokef*, and may be considered an overture to *Keser* from the *Kedusha* liturgy. *En Kitsvo* had its origin in the early 1930's, in Otwock, near Warsaw, the residence of Rabbi Saul from 1929 until the outbreak of World War II. It was sung by the Rebbe extensively. However, it is difficult to ascertain whether it was composed by the Rebbe himself or by his very ardent chasid, the famous pre-war Warsaw composer, Reb Kaufman-Idel Eidelson. This march achieved popularity among chasidim both in Poland and Galicia.

WALTZ
CD TRACK NO. 4

Tempo di valse

Modzitz

Rabbi Saul Taub, the second Rebbe of Modzitz, had a special affinity for the waltz, and some of his most beautiful melodies are in 3/4 time. This is virtually the first tune that he composed on American soil. It was composed in 1942, and given its first hearing at the wedding of his son in 1943. It was originally set to the text of Psalm 66.

MAZURKA
CD Track No. 10

Tempo di Mazurka

Modzitz

This *nigun* was composed by Kaufman-Idel Eidelson, a noted Modzitzer singer-composer, in pre-war Warsaw. In the style of a mazurka, it was sung primarily during the festival of *Purim*, often to the text of *Shoshanas Yaakov*.

ANI MAAMIN

E. D. Fastag
Text: 13 Principles of Faith

I believe with perfect faith in the coming of the
Messiah; and although he may tarry, I believe.

אֲנִי מַאֲמִין בֶּאֱמוּנָה שְׁלֵמָה
בְּבִיאַת הַמָּשִׁיחַ.
וְאַף עַל פִּי שֶׁיִּתְמַהְמֵהַּ
עִם כָּל־זֶה אֲחַכֶּה־לּוֹ
בְּכָל־יוֹם, שֶׁיָּבֹא.

Ani Maamin composed by the hasidic (Modzitz) singer-composer, Azriel Dovid
Fastag, is one of the best known songs to emerge from the Warsaw Ghetto.
According to eyewitness accounts, thousands of Jews sang this melody to the
text of *Ani Maamin* (from Maimonides' *Thirteen Articles of Faith*) as they
marched to their deaths in the gas chambers.

MUSIC OF LUBAVITCH

About twelve years after the passing of the Baal Shem Tov, Lubavitch Hasidism, also known as ChaBaD, an acronym formed from the initial letters of the words *Chochmo* [wisdom], *Binoh* [understanding] and *Da'as* knowledge], became a powerful force within Hasidism. While Chabad drew from the fountainhead of the Baal Shem Tov's philosophy, it developed its own flavor and characteristics. Rabbi Shneur Zalman of Liadi, known as the *Alter* Rebbe, founder of the Chabad movement, deepened and broadened the philosophy of Hasidism. He also discovered new depths in hasidic song. While the Baal Shem Tov revived song in Jewish life, the Alter Rebbe revealed the inner soul of hasidic melody. His ten famous melodies became the archetype of all Chabad song. Several of these "holy" songs, including the Alter Rebbe's Nigun (see page 95), are sung only at specific occasions such as the yearly *farbrengen* (get-together) on the 19th day of the Hebrew month of Kislev. This day marks the anniversary of the liberation, in 1798, of the Alter Rebbe from his imprisonment in Petersburg, Russia, after being denounced by his opponents for his activities on behalf of Hasidism. For Lubavitch, this anniversary date therefore symbolizes the victory of the Hasidic Movement over its antagonists.

The *ko'ach hanigun* (the power of melody) for Lubavitch hasidim may best be exemplified by the following anecdote. It is told that once the Alter Rebbe, Rabbi Shneur Zalman of Liadi, passed through the town of Shklov. The fame of the Rebbe had spread far and wide, and the townspeople knew he possessed a thorough knowledge of the entire Torah. The rabbis of Shklov, and the spiritual leaders from the surrounding towns, approached the Rebbe with all of the *halachic* questions that they were unable to answer in their communities. The Rebbe, however, did not respond to any of these questions. The rabbis and townspeople decided to gather in the synagogue and invited the Rebbe to give a Torah discourse after which he would answer their questions. The Rebbe accepted the invitation. When the Rebbe arrived in the cold study hall, he ascended to the lectern before the Ark and said, "Should I say Torah in order to answer your questions? No! I will sing a *nigun*." The Rebbe sang with great feeling. The study hall was hushed, and the people assembled were so absorbed in their thoughts that they did not realize where they were. While the Rebbe sang, all questions of the rabbis of *Shklov* were "answered." The hasidim believed that, with his melody, the Rebbe had opened the wells of knowledge and created a passage to the mind and intellect. All those assembled returned to their homes satisfied, and the *nigun* was known thereafter as the *Matan Torah Nigun* (The Giving of the Torah Melody).

The succeeding leaders of Lubavitch carried on the tradition of music established by Rabbi Shneur Zalman. The court of the Mitler Rebbe, Rabbi Dov Ber (son of the Alter Rebbe and second generation of Chabad leaders), had an established orchestra and choral group that inspired the Rebbe and his hasidim at various gatherings. Also, in the time of the Tsemach Tsedek, Rabbi Menachem Mendel (grandson of the Alter Rebbe and son-in- law of the Mitler Rebbe), and in the time of his son, the Rebbe Maharash (Rabbi Samuel fourth of the Chabad dynasty), hundreds of *nigunim* were composed. An especially rich period in Chabad music existed at the time of the Rebbe "Horashab" (Rabbi Sholom Dov Ber, the son of Rebbe "Maharash" and the fifth generation of the leaders of Chabad). In his famous Yeshiva, Tomchei T'mimim in Lubavitch, there was a group of musical students who dedicated themselves especially to correct singing of the Chabad *nigunim* which they collected from elderly hasidim who used to come to Lubavitch from all over the world. Rabbi Joseph Yitschok (son of the Rebbe "Horashab" and sixth leader of Chabad) emphasized in his hasidic dissertations the importance of *neginah*. After arriving on American shores in 1940, he transplanted many Lubavitcher activities to this country. The Rebbe also developed a plan to collect and perpetuate Chabad *nigunim*. In 1944, he founded the Nichoach Society whose purpose was to collect Chabad *nigunim* from various sources, determine their authentic visions, have the melodies notated and preserve them by publication in book form, and, eventually, in phonograph recordings. He appointed one of his close hasidim, Rabbi Samuel Zalmanoff, to direct these Nichoach projects. The first volume of *Sefer Hanigunim* edited by Zalmanoff, containing 175 melodies in music notation and historical background, was published in 1948. Rabbi Menachem Mendl Schneerson (son-in-law of Rabbi Joseph Yitschok and the seventh generation of Chabad leaders) also strongly encouraged the work of Nichoach. Upon his initiative, a second volume of *Sefer Hanigunim* was issued in 1957. The Rebbe instructed that a series of recordings featuring select *nigunim* of Chabad be issued. The Rebbe pointed out that spreading hasidic song was an integral part of Chabad's central mission, namely, the dissemination throughout the Jewish world of the hasidic teaching and way of life as taught by the Baal Shem Tov.

Chabad music differs considerably from general hasidic song. It is not only joyous and ecstatic, it is reflective and mystical, with a pensive and yearning quality. Chabad philosophy maintains that what is impossible to express in words may and should be conveyed in melody. While words give expression to an idea, they also limit the idea by transferring it from the spiritual realm to the physical world. Melody, in contrast, does the opposite. In song, an emotion ascends the mystical ladder of perfection, step by step to the Ultimate.

The Chabad system, first formulated by the Alter Rebbe, strives for the same goal as the other branches of Hasidism, namely the attainment of divine bliss; however, it had, and still has, a unique approach to reaching that state. For Chabad, *nigunim* were not only an integral part of Hasidism, but also a complex philosophy unto themselves. Chabad contends that it is impossible to leap immediately from extreme melancholy to extreme joy. It is impossible for a human being to rise from the lowest to the highest state without proceeding through a whole scale of the intermediate sentiments of the soul. Great stress and care is laid upon each progressive stage of development, as each is significant for the education of the soul, and for the improvement of the spirit. If one were not to go through all the stages, it would be as if someone, who had never seen the interior of a palace, were to suddenly step into its bewildering splendor. Such an individual would never be able to sense fully the glory of the palace. According to Chabad, the approach to joy, therefore, is extremely important, and each and every step must be achieved through deep meditation. Many of the Chabad *nigun*im are analyzed according to the following steps of elevation:

Hishtapchus hanefesh—the outpouring of the soul and its effort to rise out of the mire of sin, out of the *klipa*, the evil shell

Hisor'rus—spiritual awakening

Hispa'alus—the stage in which the individual is possessed by his thoughts

Dvekus—communion with God

Hislahavus—flaming ecstasy

Hispashtus Hagashmi'us—the highest state, in which the soul completely casts away its garment of flesh and becomes a disembodied spirit

---

"Melody is the outpouring of the soul. Words interrupt the stream of emotions. For the songs of the souls, when they are swaying in the high regions to drink from the well of the Almighty King, consist of tones only, dismantled of words."

—Rabbi Shneur Zalman of Liadi

THE ALTER REBBE'S NIGUN

This *nigun* regarded as the "Holy of Holies" by Lubavitcher Hasidim is known both as the *Alter Rebbe's Nigun* and the *Rav's Nigun*. According to Chabad, Rabbi Shneur Zalman of Liadi, the Alter Rebbe, composed this *nigun* in 1799, during his imprisonment in Petersburg. The *nigun* is sung by Lubavitcher Hasidim each year on the 19th day of Kislev, which commemorates the anniversary of the freeing of the Rebbe from prison. It is also sung at a weddings, bar mitzvahs, circumcisions Simchas Toroh and on other joyous occasions throughout the year. Deep content is said to be hidden in the four sections of the *nigun*, and suceeding Chabad Rebbes brought forth many explanations to enable chasidim to perceive their inner meanings. The *nigun* embodies the Rebbe's theory that melody should elevate the soul from the lowest to the highest spiritual regions. The *Alter Rebbe's Nigun* begins slowly and sounds the first stage, the outpouring of the soul. Quickly the melody begins to pick up momentum and progresses to the second stage, the spiritual awakening. The third part aims to express the steps of *hithpaaluth* and *dvekus*, until it reaches the stage of ecstasy. The fourth part presents the stage of the "disembodied soul". According to later interpretation, however, the *Alter Rebbe's Nigun* gives tonal expression to the four realms of the universe. Beginning with *briah*—the creation of the lowest elements of minerals, it moves to the second higher realm, *y'tsira*—the creation of living beings. The tune progresses to the third realm, *asiya*—the creation of man, and reaches the goal in the fourth realm, *atsiluth*—emanation, the heavenly region.

Every Chabad tune aims to voice either all the stages of elevation, or only some phases of them. Thus there are tunes expressing *dvekus*, *hishtapchus hanefesh*, *hitlahavuth*, *hisor'rus*, and so on. The last two stages are also called *Rikud*.

DER ALTER REBBES NIGUN
CD TRACK No. 6

KI ONU AMECHO
CD TRACK No. 2

Andante with feeling

כִּי אָנוּ עַמֶּךָ וְאַתָּה אֱלוֹקֵינוּ אָנוּ בָנֶיךָ,
וְאַתָּה אָבִינוּ אָנוּ קְהָלֶךָ וְאַתָּה חֶלְקֵנוּ

For we are Your people and You are our God.
We are Your children and You are our Father.

The Lubavitcher Rebbe taught this *nigun* after *Hakofos*, in 1964. He had heard it from an old hasid who sang the melody to the words of *Ki Onu Amecho* during the Yom Kippur prayers. Upon conclusion of the Fast, the old hasid had broken out in a fervent dance, singing the same melody and repeating the words again and again

OVINU MALKENU

אָבִינוּ מַלְכֵּנוּ אֵין לָנוּ מֶלֶךְ אֶלָּא אַתָּה

Our Father, our King, we have no one except You.

*Ovinu Mal*kenu is one of the ten *nigunim* composed by the Alter Rebbe, Rabbi Shneur Zalman of Liadi. The text is recited on Rosh Hashonoh, Yom Kippur, and on every Fast day; a shorter form of the prayer is read on week days on which *tachanun* (supplication) is said. The first wordless section elevates the singer to a deeply spiritual mood, the second expresses yearning for the divine, while the third is a declaration of faith in the help of our Father and King.

UFORATZTO

Vivace

Lubavitch

U - fo - ratz -to u - fo - ratz -to u - fo - ratz -to u - fo - ratz -to yo - mo vo - kéd - mo tzo-

1. fo - no vo - neg - bo___

2. fo - no vo - neg - bo___ u - fa - ratz - to

yo - mo vo - kéd - mo___ u - fa - ratz - to tzo- fo - no vo - neg - bo a- ha ha

u - fo - ratz - to u - fo - ratz -to u - fo - ratz -to u - fo - ratz -to u - fo - ratz -to

yo - mo vo - kéd - mo tso- fo - no vo - neg - bo yo - mo vo - kéd - mo tso- fo - no vo - neg -bo

וּפָרַצְתָּ יָמָּה וָקֵדְמָה
צָפוֹנָה וָנֶגְבָּה

And you shall spread forth to the west and
to the east, to the north and to the south.

Uforatzto is a theme song of the Lubavitch movement. Originally an old *nigun*, it was set to the text of Genesis 28:14 by a hasid in Israel. The numerical value of the Hebrew letters of *foratzto, pey, resh, tsadi, taf*, equals 770, the address of the Lubavitch headquarters (770 Eastern Parkway) in Brooklyn. The hasidim found extra significance in the acronym and sang *Uforatzto* with great enthusiasm. The *nigun* is also popular among other hasidic and yeshiva groups.

ELI ATA
CD TRACK No. 7

אֵלִי אַתָּה וְאוֹדֶךָ אֱלֹהַי אֲרוֹמְמֶךָ

You are my God and I will give thanks to You.
You are my God and I will exult You.

This is one of the ten *nigunim* composed by the Alter Rebbe, the founder of Lubavitch Hasidism. For many generations it has been the custom of the Lubavitcher Rebbes to sing this *nigun* at the close of the Passover *Seder*, while pouring the wine from Elijah's cup back into the decanter. The melody is set to a text from the Hallel Service recited on the Festivals. It is a heartfelt declaration of thankfulness, spiritual satisfaction, and belief in the future redemption through the coming of the Messiah.

EMOSAI KO'OSI MAR

אֵימָתַי קָאָתִי מַר לִכְשֶׁיָפוּצוּ מַעֲינוֹתֶיךָ חוּצָה

It is written that when the Baal Shem Tov's soul ascended to heaven in the year 5407, he approached the palace of the Messiah and inquired of him, "When will the Messiah come?" The Messiah answered, "I will come only when your [the *Baal Shem Tov's*] wells of Torah overflow to the outside." Lubavitch adapted a well-known melody to the text of this song, and the *nigun* is frequently sung with great ecstasy at hasidic gatherings.

HASIDIC DANCING

From time immemorial dancing was used by nations in the attempt to ward off evil spirits, threatening diseases, or droughts. Often dance served as a prelude to battle. Historically, dance was always an important and often spiritual activity within Judaism. At the Exodus, after crossing the Red Sea, Miriam, the sister of Aaron, took a timbrel in her hand and was followed by all the women with timbrels and with dancing. After the victory of Jephtah over the Ammonites, his daughter came towards him with drums and dancing. When David defeated the Philistines, the women came out from all the cities of Israel to sing and dance before King Saul. Both the Prophets and the Talmud relate how girls used to dance on the Festivals, on Tu B'av, and on Yom Kippur. At the Water Libation ceremony, held during the festival of *Sukot*, men danced before the people with torches in their hands. Throughout the Middle Ages, although beset by major problems caused by the host countries, Jews danced.

Soon after the Black Death (1348-49), an "Epidemic of Dancing" spread throughout Germany. Especially in the Rhineland, hundreds of men and women danced to utter exhaustion. Lasting until the beginning of the fifteenth century, this epidemic carried over into the Jewish ghettos, where a *Tanzhaus* (a hall for dancing) was found. Weddings took place in the *Tanzhaus*, and, during the holidays, Christian instrumentalists were permitted to play while Jews danced. Although the rabbis in Germany were not in favor of these practices, the dancing halls soon spread throughout France and Germany, until one could be found in most Jewish communities.

In Safed, Palestine, the center of Kabbalah until the year sixteen hundred, groups performed song and dance at the end of Sabbath in Jewish homes throughout the community. In addition, the older generation participated in mixed couples dancing in the style of their adoptive country. Rabbi Yehudah Hahasid attempted to put and end to this activity by decreeing that mixed dancing among the youth must cease but that religious Jewish dance by separated sexes could continue.

Rikud (dance), which can bring about ecstasy, is one of the fundamentals of Hasidism. Rabbi Nachman of Bratslav taught his followers that every part of the body had a rhythm of its own "as the melody brings out the beauty in poetry, the dance brings it to a climax." Rabbi Nachman of Bratslav, who often danced, said that the root of blessing is found in dance. His dancing was so ecstatic that Bratslaver hasidim proclaimed, "He, who did not see his dancing, saw no other good during his lifetime."

It is related among hasidim, that a Rabbi Shabtai, who lived during the time of the Baal Shem Tov, was extremely poor, and all of his weekly efforts were dedicated to obtaining minimum food necessary for the celebration of the Sabbath. Though the results of his efforts usually proved meager, Rabbi Shabtai nevertheless was joyous and sang and danced with ecstasy in honor of the Sabbath. From afar, the Baal Shem Tov was able to see Rabbi Shabtai dancing and said, "Because of his ecstatic dancing, Rabbi Shabtai will father a son who will light up the eyes of all of Israel." Shabtai's son grew up to be Rabbi Israel, the Magid of Koznitz.

Unfortunately, some of the most violent criticism leveled against hasidim by their opponents, the *misnagdim*, was the fact that they were always singing, dancing, clapping their hands, and emitting wild cries during prayers, "which is entirely against Jewish tradition." Dancing was not only encouraged by the hasidic movement but, along with song, was incorporated into religious observance and even into the liturgy. This was in keeping with the Psalmist who said, *ivdu et Hashem b'simcha* (serve God with joy). The need for joy led the Baal Shem Tov to teach his pupils not to inhibit themselves during prayers. He instructed them to move their bodies about freely, shaking and rocking from side to side, so that they could also fulfill *kol atsmosai tomarna* (all parts of my body shall proclaim), as stated in the prayer, *Nishmat*, found in the Sabbath and Festival morning liturgy.

Thus, hasidim rarely stood still during prayers, and the Rebbes and their followers injected bodily movements and actual dance steps wherever possible. These dance movements combined spontaneity with profound inner exaltation and were mainly improvised by the dancers, who expressed their individual ecstatic experiences either alone or in groups, without any intention to show off or to entertain.

There were special dances for the Sabbath, and, among the followers of the Beshtian School, it was customary for the entire village to go out, singing and dancing, to welcome the Sabbath Queen. The Sabbath Eve hymn, *L'cho Dodi* (Come My Beloved), composed by Solomon Ben Moses Halevi Alkabetz (1505-1580), was the vehicle for this mystical-devotional processional.

The singing of *L'cho Dodi* continued the tradition established by the Kabbalists of Safed who, long before the birth of Hasidism, went out every Friday afternoon in a procession over the hills of Galilee to welcome the Sabbath Queen with songs and dances. The custom of dancing during the *L'cho Dodi* has been retained in a number of hasidic synagogues to this day. This is especially true of the Bratslav hasidim, where dancing takes place not only in the synagogue, but often, during favorable weather conditions, on the street.

Dance was also at the center of the *Hakofos* (Procession of the Scrolls) on *Simchat Torah* when the Rebbe would dance wrapped in his *talis* (prayer shawl), carrying the Torah close to his heart. The Rebbe would pour out his ecstatic feelings in a rapturous dance while his followers formed a circle around him singing appropriate *nigunim* and clapping their hands rhythmically. At first, hasidic dances were performed only in the prayer-houses, but, later, such dances took place outside the synagogues for occasions such as weddings, circumcisions, or the commemoration of a notable event in the life of a beloved *Tsadik*. Hasidim who emigrated to Palestine danced annually at the grave of Rabbi Shimon Bar Yochai, a direct descendant of Moses and the author of the *Zohar*.

In some instances, hasidim indulged in rather curious customs. The followers of Rabbi Aaron of Karlin (d. 1792) used to roll on the ground in rhythm each morning before the *Shacharis* service. They were known as *kulyikes* (rollers) and were highly praised by the congregation for their devoted and saintly practice. In a moment of ecstatic fervor, some hasidim turned upside down and walked with their hands. When the fervor left them, they returned to normal walking. Dancing figured prominently in an elaborate ceremony conducted in the synagogue of the Magid of Kozhnitz when he came to pray. He entered the synagogue carrying a Torah scroll and was accompanied by two attendants bearing lighted candles. The first candle was placed near the platform and the second on the pulpit. The Rebbe then danced opposite the Holy Ark, three dance steps forward and three backward. Then he placed the little scroll into the Holy Ark and once more danced three steps forward and three backward. Only then did the Rebbe begin to pray. As he prayed, he danced with such fire and inspiration, that, when he was almost done, he fell away in a faint. Then the Rebbe, who was very frail, was wrapped in lambskin, and carried back to his private chamber, worn out and exhausted from his ecstatic dancing.

In most hasidic communities, the *mitsve tants* is the final public event of a wedding. In hasidic sources, the *mitsve tants* has a certain mystical significance and is described as a symbolic unification of a celestial bride and groom and, as a result, that of the earthly couple. The *mitsve tants* is danced to a number of traditional melodies and is directed by one individual, who invites some of the guests to dance with the bride. The bride and groom are seated and, as each guest is called, the bride stands. When the Rebbe is present, he is invited to dance first. The grandfathers dance after the Rebbe, and they are followed by the fathers and, finally, the groom. Each guest invited to dance holds one end of a kerchief or *gartle* (sash) while the bride holds the other end. As the *nigun* is sung, only the guest dances, sometimes with closed eyes, using a simple circle dance step pattern. The bride hardly moves at all, but may take a few steps when her father or bridegroom dances with her. After several steps the guest drops the sash or kerchief and is joined by the other men present, in a circle-dance, while the bride returns to her chair beside the groom. The groom is last to dance with the bride. They hold hands, take several steps, and then the groom is drawn back into the men's circle. The Rebbe does not dance the *mitsve tants* in the regular fashion. He stands in front of the bride and moves forward and backward in quick short steps. In hasidic sources, this type of dancing is called *rotso voshov* (running back and forth). This term is full of mystical connotations referring to man's attempt to come closer to God. After the dance the guests wish good luck and bid "good night" to one another and the wedding is over.

Since the Baal Shem Tov founded his movement, hasidic dancing has been performed predominantly by males. Although women would at times engage in small circle dances in a confined area, the men made dancing a prime religious activity. During the last quarter of the 20th century, *simcha* dancing, by women only, has become popular and can be seen at most traditional Jewish weddings held in Orthodox and hasidic communities. For these affairs, the dance floor is often divided by a *mechitza* (partition) so that the male and female dancing takes place in separate areas.

It is likely that *simcha* dancing developed as a reaction to women's need to dance at festive occasions. *Simcha* dancing, however, progressed and became a studied and programmed dance formula. Dance classes given by "professionals" were regularly held, and instructional videotapes, audiocassettes and compact discs made available to the market place. Borrowed primarily from American culture, such dances as the Salty Dog Rag have been adopted. Conforming to the process of adoption and adaptation, however, modification in the steps were made in order to "Judaize" these borrowed dances. While the men usually dance in large or concentric circles, the women dance singly in straight lines, and no part of their bodies come in contact with their neighbors on the dance floor.

"And it shall come to pass at the end of days, that God will make a dance for the righteous ones and He will sit among them in the Garden of Eden. And thousands of angels will grasp *kinors, nevels* and *m'tsiltayim* and every type of instruments in their hands, and they will sing at the feast. And God by himself will dance at the feast. And the sun, the moon, the stars and zodiac on his right and on his left, will dance together with Him."

—Talmud

FROM THE PROFANE TO THE HOLY

The Jewish people are a phenomenon among the nations of the world. For more than 2000 years Jews lived in those host countries that would accept and offer them citizenship or immigrant status. Arab countries, the European continent and later the Americas, served as such hosts. In some countries Jews were partially integrated and in several, they had, for a time, full rights as citizens. That a national Jewish spirit continued unabated until the return to Israel, is one of the remarkable chapters in the history of nations.

Along the way, Jews discovered an essential tool for cultural survival—the adoption of elements from their surroundings. Adopting foreign elements, however, necessitated the simultaneous act of adaptation. In keeping with the Biblical injunction *b'chukosehem lo selechu* (one must not do exactly as non-Jews do), those items that were adopted, were reworked or "Judaized." In dress, for example, certain popular and fashionable items of clothing were transformed into religious garments. Beginning in the late 18th century, hasidic leaders adopted the Polish and Russian winter fur hat. By reconstructing the hat with thirteen fur tails (corresponding to the thirteen attributes of God), the head covering became a *shtreimel*. The *shtreimel*, unlike its fur hat predecessor, was not worn casually on weekdays, but only on the Sabbath, holidays and specific celebratory events such as weddings and circumcisions. The Prince Albert style frock coat, an elegant garment popular in European society, was modified and emerged among hasidim as a *capote*. The *capote* became standard garb for many hasidic and other Orthodox Jews and is worn to this day.

For the Jewish community during the Golden Age in Spain, Hebrew remained the language of prayer and the Bible. The spoken language of the Jews, however, was Spanish with the addition of phrases borrowed from Hebrew. Known as Ladino or "Judezmo," this became the common language of Spanish Jewry and their descendants. After the Expulsion from Spain in 1492, Ladino remained a spoken language for the Jews who settled in the Mediterranean and Balkan countries. At the close of the 20th century, many Sephardic synagogues world-wide still include liturgical prayers recited in Ladino in their Sabbath and Festival services. Yiddish, another borrowed language, was based on German and contained Hebrew, Aramaic, Polish, and Russian as well as words and phrases of other languages. Yiddish was the spoken language of European Jewry and remains a viable language among those who survived the Holocaust. It is a language in which many Orthodox and hasidic Jews study the Torah and their heritage

In addition to borrowing language, dress, and ethnic foods, Jews did not hesitate to adopt foreign melodies which they added to their own long-standing musical tradition. Should Jews find the notion of adopting philosophically problematical, they should be aware that borrowing, especially in music, was not a one-way affair. From earliest times, cross-cultural borrowing of music was in place. Pope Gregory the Great (6th century AD) states in his treatise, that, when he collected and codified music for the Church (known later as Gregorian Chant), one of his primary sources was the synagogue and its music. A number of centuries later, the close relationship between Jews and Gentiles, especially during the reign of Charlemagne and his son, Louis the Pious, brought about a cultural interchange in which the Jews were more frequently the influencers than the influenced.

In 825, in a series of letters, a high Church official, Bishop Agobard, began a campaign against the Jewish influence on the Christians which, in his opinion, endangered the Christian faith. He complained that among other things, Christians attended Jewish services and preferred the blessings, prayers and music of the Jewish rabbis. It was well known that Christians attended Jewish meals on the Sabbath and were taken by the z'mirot (table songs) and that Christian women often rested on the Sabbath and worked on Sundays. Many Christians openly declared that they would like to have a lawgiver such as Moses and that the Jewish religion was the only true one. In view of these facts, Agobard demanded that no man or woman attend Jewish services, observe Sabbath, participate in Jewish festival meals, or sing their songs. Several centuries later, however, it is known that members of the Italian nobility attended Friday evening and Sabbath morning services in synagogues and brought back melodies, which they introduced into their church services.

Almost every folk music contains foreign elements. A study of French folk songs will show strains of Italian music, while Roumanian motifs can be detected in Hungarian music. Slavic influence is evident in German folk songs, and French strains appear in the music of northern Spain. The contacts between the various lands, the relationships between countries, the wars that occurred, all had a share in bringing about this musical cross-pollination and hybridization. Hasidic leaders not only allowed the borrowing of melodies from the host culture, but they advocated and urged their adherents to take secular melodies and make them "holy" by adapting them to liturgical texts for the synagogue service. They considered this act to be an exemplary *mitzvah*, that of turning the profane into the holy. The leaders felt that this was similar to turning a house of pagan worship into a synagogue. Often a Rebbe would proclaim a foreign tune worthy of being chosen for inclusion in a sacred service. He would issue instructions to redeem the *nitsotz shel k'dusha* (the spark of holiness) of the foreign folk melody and incorporate it into the repertoire of his group. It is related among the Karlin Hasidim that at the funeral of Czar Nikolai, their Tzadik, Rabbi Israel, his son and several disciples were all standing together. During the proceedings, a song was sung that the rabbi told his disciples would be worthwhile to adopt for the psalm, Mizmor Shir Chanukat Habayit (Consecration of the House). Subsequently, it was customary among the Karlin Hasidim to sing this song during the Canukah festival or when celebrating a house warming.

In addition to the adaptation of tunes from non-Jewish sources, there was internal adaptation of hasidic melodies. Often only the text was added or changed and the intact melody emerged as a new entity. (See *Hava Nagila* page 132). An interesting example of internal adaptation can be found in the popular *nigun*, *Tsiyon* (see page 111). This hasidic folk tune was originally sung with the text *Chasde Hashem ki lo somnu* found in the Sabbath *z'mira* (table song), *Boruch Hashem Yom Yom*. The lyrics, however, were changed after several yeshiva students were imprisoned for firebombing a shop selling pornography in Jerusalem. Outside the prison, a large group gathered to protest the incarceration and a student sang the *Chasde Hashem* tune to the opening line of *Tsiyon halo tishali lishlom asirayich* (O Zion, why are you not concerned with the welfare of your prisoners), a poem by the medieval Jewish philosopher Judah Halevi. The group joined in singing the *nigun* with the new lyrics. Once back in Jerusalem, the *nigun*, with the new lyrics, spread throughout the Yeshiva circles and became fully established as *Tsiyon*.

A rather fascinating postscript to this event is the adoption of *Tsiyon* by the Makuya, a Japanese Christian Zionist group. The Makuya send their young people to Israel for a period of study in various universities. The students take on Hebrew names and many spend time in a kibbutz. Years ago, the Makuya adopted *Tsiyon* as one of their theme songs. In addition to their love for Zion and Israel, the words of the refrain *ai, ai, ai, ai Tsiyon*—struck a responsive chord in the Makuya because *ai* indicates "love" in Japanese. Thus, these Christians were able to sing in Hebrew and Japanese simultaneously about their love for Zion. *Tsiyon* appears with Hebrew and Japanese lyrics in the published collection of the Makuya song repertoire.

With regard to motifs and styles, it must also be remembered that hasidim created their music in foreign cultures and that no creation can truly be called original if it does not grow in its national homeland. Only through the spiritual homeland that the hasidim created were they able

TSIYON

 צִיּוֹן הֲלֹא תִשְׁאֲלִי
לִשְׁלוֹם אֲסִירָיִךְ

O Zion why are you not concerned with the welfare of your prisoners?

to infuse an individual soul into some of these foreign currents. Later, with far less success, hasidim, notably those of Kotzk and Ger, made use of the melodies of Schubert, Chopin and Verdi. That these melodies have been completely forgotten by the hasidim is the best indication that they did not lend themselves to a reworking in the hasidic mold.

Not unlike the hasidic Rebbes, but for different motivation, the Reform Rabbinate in Germany of the 19th century urged its cantors to glean melodies from the German folk repertoire and use these tunes in the synagogue by adapting them to liturgical texts. The rabbis hoped that this borrowing would bring about a *brudershaft* (brotherhood), a common bond between the Jews and their German neighbors, through shared melodies. Thus, a number of church style hymns, such as the famous melody for *Mo'oz Tsur* (Rock of Ages), which became one of the most popular of all Jewish songs, entered the repertoire.

Many hasidic leaders felt that melodies, once used for sacred purpose, no matter how they entered the body of Jewish music, must be protected from being adopted and adapted by non-Jews. The Rebbes, therefore, prohibited the musical transcriptions of these melodies, lest they become available to the public at large and used for secular rather than religious purposes. To illustrate the power of this prohibition, hasidim relate the story of one Rebbe whose synagogue was quite different from other hasidic synagogues in Eastern Europe. This *shul* employed a professional cantor whose duties included preparing an all-male choir that would sing with him at the *Kabbolas Shabbos* (the Friday evening service). Throughout the year it was incumbent upon the cantor (let us refer to him as Reb Shlomo) to create a new melody for the *L'cho Dodi* text. Every Friday night, when cantor and choir sang this text, the Rebbe would wrap himself in a *talis* (prayer shawl) and dance throughout the rendition of the eight stanzas.

The cantor faced a rather formidable task each time he had to compose a new composition for *L'cho Dodi*. Reb Shlomo did not read music, and the tape recorder had not yet been invented. It was, therefore, extremely difficult for him to retain his newly composed melodies and harmonies. At the beginning of each week, he set out to create the new *L'cho Dodi* for the Friday night service. Sunday morning he composed the melody line to be sung by the boys. Once the melody was in place, he repeated it to himself for the better part of the day, so that he might retain it in his memory. In the evening he called in the young lads and spent several hours teaching them their parts. Before they left, Reb Shlomo made sure that they understood the need to rehearse and sing their parts back to him on Tuesday night. Bright and early on Monday morning, he would compose the music to be sung by the men, and, after repeating these melodies to himself during the day, the men were taught their parts. The members of the choir were instructed to return on Wednesday evening and be prepared to re-teach their parts to the *chaza*n if necessary.

So the week went on—Sunday, composing for the children; Sunday night, teaching the children; Monday, composing for the adults; Monday evening, teaching the adults; Tuesday, being taught back by the young lads; Wednesday, being taught back by the adults; Thursday evening was set aside for the final rehearsal, and, hopefully, they were then ready for *Kabolas Shabbos*, the Friday evening service, and *L'cho Dodi*.

A non-hasidic young man, who had moved to town and befriended the cantor, followed this weekly activity with great interest and some dismay. He knew that there must be an easier way. He suggested to his new friend that he should learn the art of *solfege* (music reading) and notation. The cantor would not hear of it because he felt that the formal study of music was not in keeping with hasidic tradition. The friend persisted, and, after several weeks, Reb Shlomo took his advice and found a musician, a short distance from town, who accepted him as a student. It was a difficult period for the cantor, but, after a great effort, he was able to master music reading and writing skills.

On the first Sunday morning that Reb Shlomo decided to use his new method, he sat down with music staff paper and spent several hours creating the new *L'cho Dodi* and writing out the choir parts. In the evening, he called in the members of the choir, taught them all their parts, and invited them to return on Thursday evening for a final rehearsal. At the final session, the cantor was able to read from his own music and correct any errors—a true pleasure! On Friday evening the choir gathered around the cantor and readied itself for the singing of the *L'cho Dodi*. Reb Shlomo hesitatingly slipped out the sheaf of music paper from underneath his prayer book, began the first tones of the melody, and had the choir join in. All eyes turned to the Rebbe, expecting to see his weekly dance. The Rebbe, however, remained seated in his chair. Something was surely wrong! Never before had the Rebbe refrained from dancing during *L'cho Dodi*. They waited with bated breath until the end of the service to hear his reason. Upon the conclusion of the service, the Rebbe said, "*Emitser hot gezindigt*" (Someone has sinned). The hasidim looked at each other with questioning eyes. Who among them could have sinned and caused the Rebbe not to dance? They looked back to the Rebbe. He pointed his finger at Reb Shlomo and said, "*Er hot gezindikt*" (he sinned). By committing this *nigun* to staff paper, the Rebbe went on to say, Reb Shlomo opened up the possibility that it would now be part of public domain and would be used by people not dedicated to holy worship.

With the exception of Abraham Zvi Idelsohn's *Thesaurus of Hebrew Oriental Melodies Vol. 10* (1933), little hasidic music found its way into print. Consequently, hundreds of hasidic *nigunim* were lost forever. The first hasidic group to overturn this prohibition against musical transcription was Lubavitch. At the instruction of the Lubavitcher Rebbe, the *Sefer Hanigunim* (1957) was issued. This collection, and the follow up *Sefer Hanigunim Volume II*, did much to preserve the important *nigunim* of Lubavitch and encourage other hasidic groups to transcribe their music. Hasidim began to believe that it was far more important to preserve the music of their group than to fear other people using it for non-religious purposes.

THE HASIDIC PARODIES

Despite its vocal opponents, that included misnagdim and maskilim, Hasidism captured the imagination and soul of the East European Jew. At the close of the nineteenth century, Hasidism numbered between three and four million adherents. At this time, however, the movement functioned in an atmosphere of abysmal poverty and bitter Czarist oppression. A number of Rebbes moved away from their primary roles as teachers and healers and became mere figureheads, surrounded by masses of followers whose blind faith they often utilized, and from whose gifts and handouts they became wealthy. The court of the Besht's grandson, Boruch Tultshiner (1780-1810), in Medzibozh was famous for its splendor and boasted its own "court jester"—Hershl Ostropoler, the hero of many folk tales. The court of Rabbi Yisroel Rizhiner (b. 1797), the founder of the Sadigura dynasty, was more like a palace in which he and his family lived. In addition to a house full of servants, he had his own band of instrumentalists and singers.

Spiritual intoxication among the hasidim would often lead to physical intoxication. The emphasis of Hasidism on joyousness often carried over to earthly pleasures of eating and drinking. Since the widespread poverty restricted such an escape from reality, however, many songs revolved around the theme of feasting and revelry.

Hasidim often abandoned themselves to such revelry, neglecting their business affairs. Others were in constant pilgrimage to their favorite Rebbe, while their families remained at home in want and hunger. The hasid sought the Rebbe's blessings and intercession with the Lord on his behalf. The Rebbe, however, could not put an end to the poverty, the persecutions, and the oppressions of the Czarist Pale. Eating and drinking, singing and dancing became tranquilizers which dulled the pain leveled at the Jewish community as a whole.

As early as the beginning of the nineteenth century, both hasidic leaders and the non-hasidic rabbinic community sensed the presence of an adversary—the *Haskalah*, the movement of Enlightenment. *Haskalah* struck a new chord in the heart of Eastern European Jews, many of whom craved the abolition of customs and practices which they believed to be founded on medieval concepts. Secular knowledge became a goal for the youth, who yearned for the freedom to read books in a foreign tongue or even in modern Hebrew.

The opponents of Hasidism began to take delight in imitating and caricaturing hasidic tunes, while utilizing satirical lyrics. These parody songs, primarily in Yiddish, were the work of the *misnagdim*, freethinkers, and others who sought to scoff at the hasidim and their leaders. Close examination, however, may lead one to understand the subconscious intent of the unknown authors of these parodies. Beyond their opposition to Hasidism, the authors of the parodies may have had a secret desire to imitate the hasidim and to savor some of the pleasures found in hasidic life—pleasures that their own group did not provide. Without such a hypothesis, it is quite difficult to understand how these misnagdim and freethinkers managed such excellent parodies within the hasidic melodic style. The tunes, created to ridicule, entered the repertoire of Yiddish folk song and have remained popular.

"Our opponents wonder at the sight of chasidim singing and dancing at their assemblies. If they understood our viewpoint, would they not become comrades?"

—Sudilkover Rebbe

UN AZ DER REBBE ZINGT

Un az der Rebbe zingt zingen ale chasidim
Un az der Rebbe tantst tantsen ale chasidim
Un az der Rebbe lacht lachen ale chasidim
Un az der Rebb shloft shlofen ale chasiidim

When the Rebbe sings, all the hasidim
sing. When the Rebbe dances all the
hasidim dance. When the Rebbe laughs
all the hasidim laugh. When the Rebbe
sleeps all the hasidim sleep.

The *misnagdim* and *maskilim* could not quite understand the strong belief that hasidim placed in their Rebbes. Nor could they understand the singing and dancing which became the hallmark of hasidic worship and festive celebrations. An unknown author penned these lyrics to a hasidic-sounding melody, and this parody became a full-fledged Yiddish folk song.

SHA, SHTIL

Sha shtil macht nit kein gereder
Der rebbi geit shoin tantzen vieder
Sha shtil macht nit kein gevald
Der rebbi geit shoin tantzen bald
Un az der rebbi tantzt tantzen mit di di vent
Lomir alle plisken mit di hent
Sha shtil ....der rebbe geit shoin singen vieder
Sha shtil.....der rebbi geit shoin singen bald
Un az der rebbi singt dem heiligen nigun
Bleibt der Soton a toiter ligen
Sha shtil....der rebbi sogt shoin Toroh vieder
Sha shtil....der rebbi sogt shoin Toroh bald
Un az der rebbi sogt far dem oilom Toroh
Hern di hasidimlach mit groiser moiroh

Quiet and be still, the Rebbe is going to dance again. And when the Rebbe dances, the walls shake. Let us all clap our hands. Quiet and be still, the Rebbe is going to sing again. And when the Rebbe sings, Satan drops dead. Quiet and be still, the Rebbe is going to discourse on Toroh. And when the Rebbe discourses on Toroh, all the hasidim listen with great fear.

Sha Shtil parodies hasidim in their singing and dancing
but the parody becomes a true Yiddish folk song.

2. Rebbiniu! Vos mein kind? Der sheigetz hot gezogt: *tut*
Ay, tut, tut is a heiliger vort tut macht talis un t'filin
Un dos is geven a malach!
3. Rebbiniu...........der sheigetz hot gezogt: *kravitz*
Kravitz? Oy, *kravitz* is a heiliger vort;
Kravitz macht *kol rino vishuo b'ohole tsadikim*, un dos.......
4. Rebbiniu! ...... der sheigetz hot gezogt: *mieshko*
Oy, *mieshko* is a heiliger vort *mieshko* meint mashke
Men darf nemen a bisele mashke, un dos is geven a malach,

Some unknown author lightheartedly, but perhaps admiringly, proves.
how a hasidic Rebbe can interpret a common question in a thoroughly
Jewish way in this well-known parody song.

A mystified Jew runs to his Rebbe to find out the meaning of a
mysterious sentence that he heard a non-Jew say when knocking at his
door. He relates to the Rebbe that he distinctly heard the words, *Tzi tut
kravitz mieshko,* but did not know what the words meant. The Rebbe
easily explains that an angel said these words. The numerical value of
the letters of *Tzi* is 101, which means that the Torah must be studied
101 times. *Tut* is an abbreviation for *talis un tfilin* (praying shawl and
phylacteries). *Kravitz* is the abbreviation for "*Kol rino vishu'o b'ohole
tsadikim*" (found in the Hallel Service recited on Festivals), which
indicates that the Torah must be studied in the tents of the righteous.
Mieshko should be understood as *Mashke*—liquor. Therefore,
according to the Rebbe, the mystifying words clearly mean, that the
Torah must be studied 101 times in the tents of the righteous while
wearing *talis* and *t'filin* and drinking a little whiskey. The literal
meaning of the Polish words, however, is, *does the tailor live here?*

NEO HASIDIC SONG

The most lasting influence on hasidic melodies in the latter half of the 20th century, must be credited to Rabbi Shlomo Carlebach. In his efforts to bring back those who strayed from the path of traditional Judaism, Shlomo traveled the world beginning in the late 1950's, presenting his original melodies and stories in synagogues, schools, community centers, summer camps and other organizations. Because his songs often did not adhere strictly to the melodic or rhythmical characteristics of Eastern European chassidic song, many listeners felt that his music could at most be labeled *shir dati* (religious song) or neo-hasidic song.

Carlebach's first of many recordings, *Hanshomo Loch*, (Zimrani Records, New York, 1961) featured twelve songs, and was arranged and conducted by Milt Okun, a well-known musician who was active in the field of popular American music. Okun had been the long-time arranger for the acclaimed folk singer, Harry Belafonte. *Hanshomo Loch* proved to be very popular, especially with a large segment of American Jewish youth. The contemporary sounds of the melodies and the background arrangements were perceptibly different from those that had heretofore been considered "traditionally Jewish."

To Shlomo Carlebach belongs the distinction of being the first to take the *nigun* out of its usual habitats, the synagogue, *z'mirot*, the *farbrengen*, weddings, bar mitzvahs and to present it, accompanied by guitar and other instruments, in concert. Much of his musical output including *Esa Enai* (see page 123), *Od Yishama, V'haer Enenu, Uva'u Ha'ovdim*, and *Am Yisrael Chai* were first presented at these concerts and thereafter introduced by Shlomo to Jews in far-flung communities world-wide.

On the heels of Shlomo Carlebach followed the Rabbis' Sons, a performing group of four religiously observant young men trained in

American yeshivas. The Rabbis' Sons appeared on stages in many major cities during the late 1960's and early 1970's, and their exposure to contemporary music was evident in much of their original song repertoire. An example of this contemporary musical influence can be heard in the opening tones of *Mi Ho'ish* (See page 126), recorded in 1967. Although the opening section was unusual for a hasidic melody, the song nevertheless entered into and became part of the hasidic and yeshiva repertoire, where it has remained to this day.

The public performances of Shlomo Carlebach and the Rabbis' Sons laid the groundwork for several other groups whose concerts spawned a host of new recordings featuring melodies set to liturgical texts. The music, composed and performed by the various groups, succeeded in satisfying the musical tastes of the younger generation, and it became their *gebrauch* (all-purpose) as well as religious music. As the recordings and concerts proliferated, most other Jews began to accept these new *nigunim*.

At the same time, in order to satisfy the needs of the hasidic community who needed the older Eastern European hasidic music, recordings of *Modzitz, Ger, Lubavitch, Vishnitz, Belz, Bobov* and other hasidic "courts" were produced. However, influenced by contemporary music, these recordings were given modern sounding instrumental backgrounds.

Perhaps the widest recognition of the newer hasidic music can be attributed to the first Israeli Chasidic Song Festival presented in Tel Aviv in November, 1969. Held as an open music competition, the Festival was later performed in the major cities of Israel. The phonograph recording of the Festival music issued under the *Hed Arzi* label, became a worldwide success, as evidenced by one of its best known songs, "*Ose Shalom*" (See page127). This song, set to liturgical text, topped Israel's popular song charts and became familiar to Jews throughout the world.

The subsequent yearly Chasidic Song Festivals and their recordings, as well as the international concerts of various troupes, provided hasidic music with a completely new image and an appeal to a broad segment of the Jewish public. However, many Jews, nurtured on the hasidic music of Eastern Europe, still had difficulty in accepting the newer nigunim. Often, and with passion, they proclaimed that many of the newer songs lacked the depth, feeling, and intent of traditional nigunim. In addition, they pointed to the rather limited life span enjoyed by most of these melodies. They claimed that these songs had become part of a "hasidic hit parade," and would be discarded and forgotten after a period, in favor of newer tunes.

As the neo-hasidic music was performed and recorded by Shlomo Carlebach, The Rabbis' Sons, Mordechai Ben David, Avrom Fried, the Pirchei Boys Choir, Dveykus, Miami Boys Choir and others, its popularity began to soar. Those who loved "authentic" hasidic song felt that many of these newer nigunim had been commercialized by "pop singers" who often appeared on concert stages with costumed boys' choirs and large bands playing disco beat. These concerts came to be looked upon by many as entertainment, rather than events in which spiritually moving liturgical songs were presented.

On the other hand, many neo-hasidic songwriters insisted that they were well within hasidic tradition. They believed that, just as the musical forms of peasant dances, waltzes, marches, and shepherds' melodies were adopted by Jews from their European surroundings, the new hasidic music incorporated the melodic and rhythmical elements of American, Israeli, Jazz, Country and Rock. In addition, they liked to quote from hasidic Masters, including Rabbi Nachman of Bratslav, who stated that "all music emanates from the Hechal Han'gina (the Temple of Music). Because music is divinely inspired, it does not contain impurities, and all music may be utilized." And so it goes on. Jews continue to adopt sounds, motifs and musical styles of their surrounding culture. It is difficult to avoid such influences while living in open societies. To the tribute of the creators of the new Jewish religious songs, however, the musical elements adopted were also adapted. Thus, new Jewish melodies did not remain static but became part of the evolution of a Jewish musical tradition

ESO ENAI
CD TRACK No. 5

Moderately   S. Carlebach

אֶשָּׂא עֵינַי אֶל הֶהָרִים
מֵאַיִן יָבוֹא עֶזְרִי
עֶזְרִי מֵעִם יְיָ
עוֹשֵׂה שָׁמַיִם וָאָרֶץ

I lift up my eyes to the hills. Whence comes my help? My help is from the Lord, Creator of heaven and earth.

Possibly the best-known song of Rabbi Shlomo Carlebach, *Eso Enai* was recorded in 1961 on *Han'shomo Loch* (Zimrani Records). *Eso Enai*, and dozens of additional melodies created by Shlomo Carlebach, have become a permanent part of the Jewish musical repertoire.

ETZ CHAYIM HI
CD TRACK No. 9

Music: T. Portnoy   Lyrics: liturgy

che - ha dar - ché no - am v' - chol n' -

ti - vo - te ha sha - lom_____

כִּי לֶקַח טוֹב נָתַתִּי לָכֶם
תּוֹרָתִי אַל תַּעֲזוֹבוּ
עֵץ חַיִּים הִיא לַמַּחֲזִיקִים בָּה
וְתֹמְכֶיהָ מְאֻשָּׁר
דְּרָכֶיהָ דַרְכֵי נֹעַם
וְכָל נְתִיבוֹתֶיהָ שָׁלוֹם

I give you good instruction; forsake not my Torah. It is a tree of life to those who take hold of it, and happy are those who support it. Its ways are the ways of pleasantness, and all the paths are peace. Turn us to You, O Lord, and let us return; renew our days as of old.

This is an example of a neo-hasidic song that has been incorporated into the liturgy in synagogues word-wide. The *Etz Chayim* text is either read or sung at the end of the Torah service when the Scrolls are placed back into the ark. Although one of its musical phrases is reminiscent of an internationally known song, this melody by Tanchum Portnoy has become part of the Jewish repertoire.

MI HO'ISH
CD TRACK No. 15

Music: B. Chait Lyrics: Liturgy

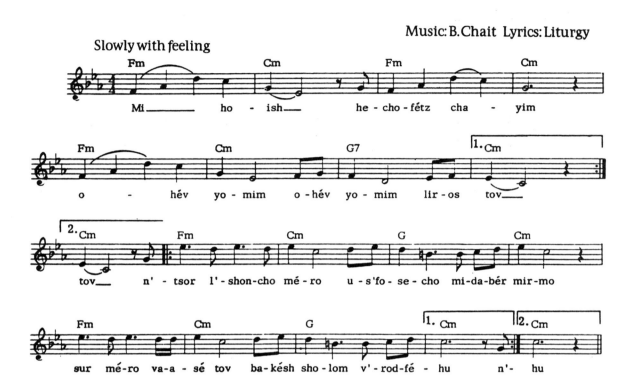

מִי הָאִישׁ הֶחָפֵץ חַיִּים, אֹהֵב יָמִים לִרְאוֹת טוֹב
נְצֹר לְשׁוֹנְךָ מֵרָע, וּשְׂפָתֶיךָ מִדַּבֵּר מִרְמָה
סוּר מֵרָע וַעֲשֵׂה טוֹב, בַּקֵּשׁ שָׁלוֹם וְרָדְפֵהוּ

Who is the man that desires life? Keep your
tongue from evil, seek peace and pursue it.

Mi Ho'ish first appeared on the recording "The Rabbis' Sons in 1967."
For a number of years, The Rabbis' Sons (comprised of four young men)
brought their original compositions to Jewish audiences throughout the
United States. Several additional recordings of their original melodies
were issued.

OSE SHALOM

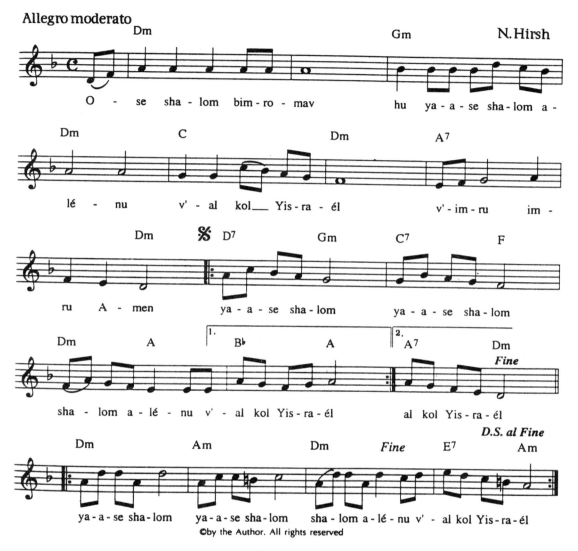

עֹשֶׂה שָׁלוֹם בִּמְרוֹמָיו
הוּא יַעֲשֶׂה שָׁלוֹם עָלֵינוּ
וְעַל כָּל יִשְׂרָאֵל וְאִמְרוּ אָמֵן

May He who makes peace in the high places make
peace for Israel and for all mankind and say Amen.

Ose Shalom was presented in 1969 at the first Israeli Chasidic
Song Festival held in Tel Aviv. The recorded version was used as
background music for Israeli Tourism commercials. *Ose Shalom*
became a "traditional" congregational melody in many synagogues
throughout the world.

YIDEN

A late 20th century rock song, *Genghis Khan*, was entered in the Eurovision Song Festival competition. It appeared soon after with Yiddish lyrics which joyously proclaim the coming of the Messiah. At traditional Jewish *simchas, Yiden* is danced by both men and women , although in separate areas and with different steps.

Vivace

Melodies, Stories & Annotations

HAVA NAGILA

If there is one song that represents Jewish music to the world at large, it is most certainly *Hava Nagila*. This song was taken out of the limited sphere of Jewish music and entered the body of world folk music. Major folk singers, classic artists and ensembles including Harry Belafonte, Miriam Makeba, Odetta, Sammy Davis Jr., Richard Tucker, The London Symphony Orchestra, among others, have recorded *Hava Nagila*. In the United States, especially, one can hear piped in versions of this melody in restaurants, public elevators and hotel lobbies, during seventh inning stretches at baseball games, between periods in hockey, and for musical interludes at events like the Democratic and Republican National Conventions.

Contrary to popular belief, *Hava Nagila* is not an Israeli tune but a *nigun* composed in the hasidic court of Sadigora, Poland. During the early part of the twentieth century, the renowned Jewish musicologist, Dr. Abraham Zvi Idelsohn, transcribed, analyzed and annotated melodies from the diverse Jewish communities living in Palestine. Using a cylinder device, the precursor of modern day recording equipment, he recorded liturgical, Yiddish, hasidic, choral, and children's lullabies from the Ashkenazic and Sephardic-Oriental communities. His research, analysis and transcriptions culminated with the publication of the ten-volume *Thesaurus of Hebrew/Oriental Melodies*, regarded as the definitive work in 20th century Jewish musicology. The *Thesaurus* can be found in music and academic libraries throughout the world. In *Volume IX*, Idelsohn offers the following information regarding the *Hava Nagila* tune:

> This song may serve as an example of how a song becomes a popular folk song, and particularly how a song becomes Palestinian. The tune originated at the court of Sadigora

(Bokowina) and was brought to Jerusalem. In 1915, I wrote it down. In 1918, I needed a popular tune for a performance of a mixed choir in Jerusalem. My choice fell upon this tune which I arranged in four parts and for which I wrote a Hebrew text. The choir sang it and apparently caught the imagination of the people, for the next day men and women were singing the song throughout Jerusalem. In no time, it spread throughout the country, and thence throughout the Jewish world. In 1921, I printed the song, in my arrangement, in my Hebrew songbook *Sefer Hashirim*, page 164-165. Since then, it has been printed in several songsters as Palestinian.

There are those who have disputed Idelsohn with regard to the authorship of the *Hava Nagila* lyrics. Several former students of the late Moshe Nathanson, a well-known Israeli cantor, musician and educator, claimed that the information given them by their teacher contradicted Idelsohn. Nathanson, they said, agreed that Idelsohn had introduced the Sadigora *nigun*, but that it was he, Nathanson, who had written the lyrics. This occurred, they said, when he was a young student in Idelsohn's music classes held in Jerusalem. The seven rather simplistic Hebrew words which make up the lyrics, whether written by Idelsohn or Nathanson, helped propel the *nigun* into one of the world's best known folk songs.

"Every locksmith has a master key with which he can open many doors. *Neginah* is such a key, for it can unlock all doors."

—Sayings of Chabad

HAVA NAGILA

הָבָה נָגִילָה וְנִשְׂמְחָה
עוּרוּ אַחִים בְּלֵב שָׂמֵחַ

Come let us be glad and rejoice. Arise brethren, with a joyful heart.

MISERLOU
"A HOLY NIGUN"

In mid 1969, after receiving a sabbatical and a small research grant, I prepared to spend a year in Israel with my family. Prior to our departure, I received a tape recording from Jerusalem with melodies of the Bratslav Hasidim. Because of my previous involvement in hasidic music recordings, I was known as an "expert" in this genre. The Bratslaver Hasidim, therefore, requested my advice regarding *nigunim* they hoped to sing in a forthcoming recording project. I listened to the tape, made some notes, and wrote several suggestions. Just before the reel ended, I heard a group of men singing an internationally known melody, *Miserlou*, which I knew to be a folk tune originating in the Mediterranean basin. My first reaction on hearing this melody was to think that the tape sent to me had not been properly erased before the Bratslav Hasidim began to record their *nigunim*. I conveyed this thought in writing to the Bratslav head office in Jerusalem. In their response, the hasidim were quick to hint that my knowledge of hasidic music was less than "expert." The *melody,* they said, was sung in Bratslav for generations and was a "holy *nigun.*" I was very puzzled, and told myself that they were privy to information that I did not have.

I arrived in Israel during the first days of October in 1969, and looked forward with great anticipation to a fruitful year of collecting and annotating hasidic music. I hoped that I would gather enough material to complete a second volume of *Songs of the Chassidim*. Within a month of my arrival, I received a telephone call from Rabbi Meir Shimon Geshuri, the director of the Jerusalem *Machon L'musika Datit* (the Institute for Religious Music). Rabbi Geshuri, the acknowledged expert in hasidic music, had created a large catalog of *nigunim*. I was truly flattered when he asked me to look through this catalog and correct musical transcriptions and authorship as I deemed necessary. Towards the end of the Fall, I spent several days in the Institute scrutinizing transcriptions spread over several hundred index cards. Each card contained the first four bars of a melody and the name of the hasidic group from which it originated. The inaccuracies that I found early on were primarily in the incorrect authorship given to melodies composed by Rabbi Shlomo Carlebach. In addition, I felt that a number of melodies had not been transcribed as they were commonly sung. I noted these, gave the proper authorship, and continued with the cards.

After several hours perusing the cards, I picked up one that contained the first four bars of *Miserlou*, with credit for the tune given to Bratslav. I took the card to Rabbi Geshuri and told him that this was my second encounter with the "Bratslav tune." When I asked him why its authorship was assigned to these hasidim, he simply shrugged his shoulders and said to me in Yiddish, *"ich veys nisht"* (I do not know) and went on with his work. The little mystery of *Miserlou* remained unsolved.

A month later, I received a telephone call from the music library at Hebrew University in Jerusalem. Would I volunteer my services for their music catalog as I had for the Institute? I found it difficult to refuse the invitation, and two weeks later I again found myself in Jerusalem studying hundreds of cards. During my third afternoon, I found a notation of *Miserlou* credited to Bratslav. I showed it to Dr. Avigdor Herzog, the director of the Phonoteka (music archives), and informed him that this was the third time I had come across this "Bratslav *nigun*." We both knew with certainty that it was not a hasidic melody. Why then was it being credited to Bratslav? He pointed to an asterisk next to the *nigun*. Following the asterisk to the bottom of the card, I saw the words *Shirei Meron* (Songs of Meron). Dr. Herzog informed me that on the seventh day of the Hebrew month *Adar*, the *yahrzeit* (anniversary of death) of Moses is commemorated in the Galilee town of Meron several miles from the city of Safed. It is stated in the Bible that God took Moses away and that his burial place is unknown. It had, therefore, never been possible to have a gravesite commemoration in his memory. Hasidim of Bratslav were aware that, according to legend, Meron is the burial place of Rabbi Simon Bar Yochai, a direct descendant of Moses. They felt that the crypt site of Rabbi Simon would therefore be the best place to honor the memory of Moses. Beginning in the early part of the 20th century, hundreds of Bratslav Hasidim, along with klezmer musicians, came to Meron each year on this anniversary to celebrate with song and dance the greatest leader of the Jewish people.

Several musicians and acquaintances encouraged me to be in Meron at the *yahrzeit* where I might possibly solve the mystery of *Miserlou.* In 1970, the seventh day of *Adar* fell on a Saturday evening. Because of the hazard of nighttime driving on the Galilee roads, we elected to stay in Safed for Shabbat and to travel the short distance to Meron after *Havdalah,* the closing ceremony of the Sabbath. We arrived at the crypt site in the early evening and waited for the hasidim to arrive. Those from the northern part of the country arrived first; those living in the southern part of the country came last. By 11 o'clock, the festivities were in full swing, with several hundred hasidim in attendance. The singing picked up; the dancing was exhilarating; and I waited anxiously with my portable recording equipment ready for *Miserlou.* At 1a.m. the great moment arrived, and hasidim began to sing the melody with vocalized *ya ba ba ba bai bai* syllables. At last, my research was at hand! The first hasid I questioned told me that this *nigun* was part of the Bratslav musical repertoire since the turn of the century. The second, third, and fourth provided me with similar information. My frustration was growing, and I feared that my musicological query might remain unanswered. Several more attempts elicited the same responses. The singing was beginning to abate when I saw a rather tall, distinguished looking hasid. I immediately approached him and asked if he could give me any information about this *nigun.*

"Why do you ask?" he said.

I informed him that I did research and recording in hasidic music.

"You are the first to ask," he responded.

"Since I am the first to ask, please allow me also to be the first to know," I said.

He motioned that I should follow him out of the crypt area.

"Did you study in a yeshiva in the United States?" he asked.

"Yes," I replied.

"Then this should be rather easy for you," he continued. "Until 1948 a group of Druse elders attended this annual celebration in Meron.

"I haven't the slightest idea," I responded.

"No, no. Think," he said.

"I can't," was my reply.

"But you went to a yeshiva!"

"Please do not test my Judaic knowledge at this time of the morning," I begged.

"All right," he said, "the Druse are descended from whom?"

"From Jethro," I said.

"And who was Jethro?" he asked.

"The father-in-law of Moses," I replied.

My hasidic informant continued to explain that Rabbi Shimon Bar Yochai is therefore a descendant of Jethro as well as Moses. Because it was extremely difficult to get to the burial place of Jethro, the Druse accepted the Bratslav rationale and elected to come to the crypt site of Rabbi Shimon Bar Yochai. There they gave honor to their ancestor, Jethro, at the burial site of one of his descendants. "And so it came to pass that Jews and Druse stood side by side at the crypt of Rabbi Shimon Bar Yochai, honoring their respective ancestors," said my Bratslaver hasid. "Picture this crypt site," the hasid continued. "Several hundred hasidim were singing and dancing while the Druse elders waited patiently on the side. When the Bratslaver hasidim were spent, the relaxed Druse elders jumped in and begin singing and dancing to one of their own melodies, *Miserlou*. Several Bratslaver hasidim found the melody quite Jewish-sounding and joined hands with the Druse."

I learned from my hasid that, in the following years, more Bratslaver Hasidim joined in dancing with the Druse during the Meron celebration. Following the Israel War of Independence in 1948, the Druse stopped coming to Meron and never returned. *Miserlou*, however, remained part of the celebration and became a "Bratslaver *nigun*" acquiring the status of "holiness" and historicity. This adoption was rather easy to accomplish because the melody is in an Eastern European modality very close to the "Jewish ear." Along the way Bratslav Hasidim introduced this "holy nigun" to other Jews and it became known in a number of hasidic circles. Today, one will often hear this melody played at traditional Jewish weddings. If one were to inquire about the origins of this melody, the answer would most probably be a "holy hasidic *nigun*."

"Many a melody once chanted by the Levites in
the Holy Temple is now in exile among the
unlearned, common people."
—Rabbi Yitzchok of Kalev

MISERLOU
CD TRACK No. 13

Moderately

NAPOLEON'S MARCH

In the early 1970's, I attended my first Lubavitch wedding reception at the Brooklyn Jewish Center. This establishment had once housed one of the largest and most influential Conservative synagogues and Hebrew schools in the metropolitan New York area. Richard Tucker, the internationally acclaimed tenor, served this synagogue as its cantor for several years before he joined the Metropolitan Opera. Due to demographic changes in the immediate bordering area of Crown Heights, however, the Center was transformed into a facility for weddings, bar mitzvahs, and other festive events of the Lubavitcher Hasidim.

The *dvekus* (slow rapturous melody) which accompanied the groom as he walked down the aisle to the *chupah* (wedding canopy) was truly inspirational. "This beautiful melody is the *Alter Rebbe's Nigun*" (see page 95), I was informed. Several weeks later, at another ceremony, the Lubavitcher hasidim sang a stirring march as the bridegroom was led to the canopy. After inquiring, I was given the name of this melody, *Napoleon's March*. I thought it rather ludicrous that hasidim could entertain the thought of singing a melody bearing such a title. After the wedding, I researched the origins of the tune and it's seemingly strange title and discovered its importance to the hasidim of Lubavitch.

In 1812, Napoleon and his army were on their ill-fated trek towards Moscow. When the army was scheduled to pass by the town of Lubavitch, hasidim went out to greet Napoleon. There were many who believed that he might be a savior of the Jews. The hasidim heard the military bands on parade and were captivated by their marching tunes. They were able to learn several of them, and, upon their return to Lubavitch, sang one of these melodies to the Alter Rebbe. The Rebbe proclaimed the melody to be a "*shir nitzochon*" (a song of victory) and asserted that it possessed a *nitzotz shel k'dusho* (a spark of holiness).

He asked the hasidim to teach it to their Lubavitcher brethren and instructed them to sing the march melody during the *Neila* service on Yom Kippur, just before the *shofar* blast which ends the Fast. The custom of singing *Napoleon's March* at *Neila* was kept in all Lubavitcher synagogues and continues to the present.

To be sure, if members of Napoleon's army core were resurrected by some miracle and able to listen to the Lubavitcher, they would be mystified by the rendition of their marching song. This melody, when sung by hasidim, no longer captures the spirit of Napoleon's army. It is rather a *nigun* filled with the deep feelings and pathos of the hasid who has been told, and believes it to be, a holy song. Although identical, note for note to *Napoleon's March*, the melody has been infused with the "spark of holiness." In Lubavitch, *Napoleon's March*, has truly become a *shir shel nitzachon*, a song of victory.

"All melodies well forth from the fountain of holiness, from the Palace of Music."

—Zohar

NAPOLEON'S MARCH
CD TRACK No. 14

Majestically

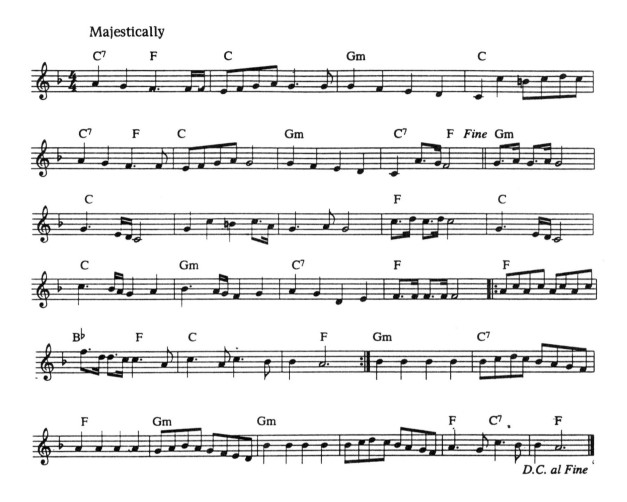

D.C. al Fine

NYE ZURITSE CHLOPTSI
CD TRACK No. 12

This song, a favorite of the Lubavitch Hasidim, was adopted from the Ukrainian peasant repertoire. When it was first recorded in 1962, Rabbi Shmuel Zalmanoff, the Lubavitcher music consultant, translated the song's Ukrainian lyrics for me: "Don't worry fellows about what will become of us; when you come to the inn, you will find plenty of vodka to drink." I was slightly mortified by the knowledge that I was scheduled to conduct a drinking song on the first recording of Lubavitch music.

"Why would any one want to put a song about vodka on a recording of Lubavitch music?" I asked.

Rabbi Zalmanoff dismissed my question by informing me that non-hasidim could often be *klein kepeldik* (small in the cranial region). Should I make the effort to think like a hasid for just a few moments, he would give me the true meaning of this very important text. After I agreed, Rabbi Zalmanoff suggested three substitutions, (a) Jewish brothers, (b) God, (c) material needs. The hasidic interpretation of the lyrics immediately became evident "Don't worry Jewish brothers (fellows), *God* (the inn) will take care of all your material needs (vodka).

"Why in the world don't you sing it with these words?" I asked.

Rabbi Zalmanoff informed me that it was important to understand the sociological condition of Jews in Russia at the time of the Miteler Rebbe, the second Rebbe of Lubavitch. The Russian government frowned upon Torah and other Judaic studies. Nevertheless, classes were held and students studied underground, though at great risk. The rabbis taught a number of songs, including drinking songs, to their students, and infused the non-Jewish lyrics with religious meaning. When hasidim, posted outside the makeshift classrooms, informed the teachers that the Cossacks were coming through town, the students were told to hide their holy books quickly. They were then led by their teachers in a merry rendition of one of these songs, having been taught the "true" meaning of the words previously.

"Imagine the delight of the Cossacks when they heard the young students singing their drinking song," said Rabbi Zalmanoff.

During the time of the Miteler Rebbe, *Nye Zuritse Chloptsi* became the unofficial traveling song sung by hasidim on their way to and from Lubavitch. It is still sung with great gusto, in the original Ukrainian, during Lubavitch *farbrengen* worldwide.

LE MARSEILLES
The French National Anthem

When Georges Pompidou served as premier of France, the relationship between his country and the State of Israel almost reached bottom. Several months after Pompidou's death, I attended a Lubavitch wedding in the Brooklyn Jewish Center. As is customary among hasidim, men and women were separated both during the meal and on the dance floor. I was happily seated with members of my chorus who participated in the first phonograph recording of Lubavitcher music.

The band played Lubavitcher and other hasidic melodies continuously, and, just before the meal ended, I was shocked to hear *Le Marseilles*, the French national anthem. Within moments, men and women were out of their seats scurrying to their respective sections of the dance floor. It was truly memorable to see the dancing and hear this melody sung with *yai dai dai* syllables. I could not contain myself and broke into laughter. My researcher's instinct told me that there had to be a very good reason for the *Marseilles*. Each hasid that I questioned identified the tune in identical manner, "a holy Lubavitcher *nigun*." Almost in desperation, I approached a ten-year-old Lubavitcher boy.

"Do you know the song everyone is singing?" I asked

He looked up at me and repeated the now familiar words, "A holy Lubavitch *nigun*."

"This is the national anthem of France!" I said emphatically.

"Don't believe it!" he said as he pointed his index finger at me.

I have yet to find anything more disconcerting than being put down by a ten-year-old Lubavitcher hasid. In frustration, I continued to ask, only to hear the phrase, "a holy Lubavitcher *nigun*" repeated. In my final attempt of the evening, I asked an older hasid for information.

"I don't know too much about this *nigun*," he said, "but I do know that the day after they began singing this melody in Lubavitch, Georges Pompidou dropped dead."

"You can't be serious," I shot back.

"I only know that it happened," he said.

"How wonderful!" I thought. Jews now have a potent weapon. They can simply sing a *nigun* and make their enemies disappear.

I left the wedding hall quite annoyed at not having found a satisfactory reason for the Lubavitcher hasidim and the *Marseilles*. With my annoyance, however, also came a determination to discover the true reason. It took several weeks, but, when I found the answer, it was quite moving in its simplicity.

Lubavitcher hasidim hold their annual *Hakofos*, on the holiday of *Simchas Toroh*, in their main synagogue located in the Crown Heights section of Brooklyn. Late one *Simchas Toroh* evening, several young men entered the main Lubavitch Synagogue. The Rebbe noticed them and sent one of his hasidim to find out who they were. The hasid reported that they were Jewish students from the Sorbonne University in Paris. The Lubavitcher Rebbe, who had himself studied at the Sorbonne, knew immediately how to greet these students in a meaningful manner. He asked hasidim sitting close by who knew the *Marseilles* to sing the anthem. All eyes turned towards the dais as the students were escorted to the Rebbe and his personal welcome.

After the holiday, Lubavitcher hasidim recalled that the Rebbe had asked that the *Marseilles* be sung. The anthem was introduced again at subsequent Lubavitch gatherings but now formally set to a liturgical poem, *Ho'aderes v'ho-emuno*, found in the Sabbath and Festival morning service. In the years since then, the melody has become a permanent part of the Lubavitcher musical repertoire. It is quite conceivable that, at some future date, Lubavitcher hasidim may unwittingly believe that the French borrowed this melody from them.

THE SONG OF THE ROOSTER
SZOL A KAKAS MAR

Rabbi Isaac Taub, the *Tzadik* of Kalev (1748?-1800), took upon himself a sacred mission of "saving" melodies from the non-Jewish milieu that could be used in Jewish celebration and worship. Rabbi Taub lived in a Transylvanian locale where shepherds grazed their sheep and rounded them up with melodies played on flute-like instruments. Once a month, Rabbi Taub, together with his *shamash* and *gabbai* (synagogue assistants), would dress in shepherds' clothing and travel to the grazing area for the express purpose of *rateven a nigun* (saving a melody). On one such foray, the Rebbe heard a gentile shepherd play a particularly appealing melody. He asked the shepherd to teach him the tune. According to hasidic lore, after the Rebbe learned the melody, he put his hand into his pocket, drew out several coins and gave them to the shepherd, thereby "buying" the *nigun*. In a variation of this story, as soon as the Rebbe learned the melody, he took his walking cane and tapped the shepherd gently on the head. The shepherd immediately "forgot" the melody, and it became a Kalev *nigun*.

I had been relating these two versions for many years and one evening, following a public lecture, a Hungarian émigré informed me that both were wrong. The version he knew, although similar to the other two, was doubly beautiful. When the *Tzadik* of Kalev had learned the tune, he snapped the shepherd on the upper lip and the shepherd forgot the melody. This echoes the well-known *Midrash* that the angels teach all Jews the Torah and wisdom of the world while they are in their mother's womb. At birth, an angel, known as the *Malach Hashikcha* (the Angel of Forgetfulness), snaps the child on the upper lip, leaving a small indent, and all Torah and wisdom is forgotten. Subsequently, it is the sacred duty of every Jew to regain this knowledge throughout life. The Rebbe of

Kalev acted as the *Malach Hashikcha*, causing the shepherd to forget the melody. Thus the Rebbe acquired the melody for the Jewish people.

The Rebbe of Kalev returned home, and, during a *tish*, taught the melody with its Hungarian lyrics, "The rooster is already crowing, the sun will soon rise." The hasidim were perplexed and wondered why their Rebbe would sing about a rooster crowing at dawn? When asked, the Rebbe explained that this song was not about a rooster crowing at dawn, but about the dawn of the Messiah. The hasidim, who believed fervently in their spiritual leader, never doubted that the Rebbe's interpretation was correct. In order to add to the religious meaning for the hasidim, an additional line in Hebrew and Hungarian, *Adonenu r'ey v'onyenu miert ninch az marv* (Our Lord see our affliction, why does he, the Messiah, not yet come?), was added to the original lyrics.

In the years following the adoption of this melody, additional and somewhat lengthy Yiddish and Hebrew lyrics were added. At the close of the 20th century, Hungarian hasidim sing this melody on special occasions, holidays, and at traditional Jewish weddings.

The rooster is already crowing, the sun will soon rise. Our Lord see our affliction, why does he (the Messiah) not yet come?

szol a ka-kas már

maid megvirad mar

אֲדוֹנֵנוּ רְאֵה בְּעָנְיֵנוּ.

miert ninch az márv

"THE SONG OF THE ANGELS"
LO'EL ASHER SHOVAS

The attribution of heavenly origins for specific melodies incorporated into the repertoire of *nigunim*, was common to a number of hasidic groups. For the hasidic leaders it was not an issue that a number of these "melodies from heaven" had similar tunes in the non-Jewish folk repertoire of Europe. Among the hasidim of the *Choze* (Seer), of Lublin, *Lo'el Asher Shovas* was known as *The Song of the Angels*. According to hasidic lore, the *Choze* closed his eyes during the *tish* (table gathering) one Friday evening. The hasidim could only assume that their Rebbe had fallen asleep or had entered a trance-like stage. When the *Choze* opened his eyes, he proclaimed that he had ascended to heaven. During his stay there, he said, the angels taught him *Lo'el Asher Shovas*. He proceded to teach the *nigun* to the hasidim who learned it quickly. All those assembled accepted *Lo'el Asher Shovas* as a "holy nigun." To this day, it is a mainstay in the Sabbath song repertoire of the *Choze*'s descendants, among them the hasidim of Ropshitz, Sanz and Bobov.

"It is said that the Mansion of Song and the Mansion of Penitence are close to each other, and I say that the Mansion of Song is the Mansion of Penitence."

—Rabbi Yisroel of Modzitz

LOEL ASHER SHOVAS

"Choze" of Lublin

Majestically

Lo - él a - sher___ sho - vas mi - kol ha - ma - a - sim

mi ___ kol ___ ha - ma - a - sim u - va - yōm ___

ha - sh' - vi - i nis - a - lo v' - yo - shav al ki - se ch' - vō - dō

tif - e - res ___ o - to l' - yōm ___ ham - nu - cho

o - neg ko - ro l' - yōm ha - Sha - bos

לָאֵל אֲשֶׁר שָׁבַת מִכָּל הַמַּעֲשִׂים בַּיּוֹם הַשְּׁבִיעִי;
הִתְעַלָּה וְיָשַׁב עַל כִּסֵּא כְבוֹדוֹ;
תִּפְאֶרֶת עָטָה לְיוֹם הַמְּנוּחָה,
עֹנֶג קָרָא לְיוֹם הַשַּׁבָּת.

To God who rested from all the work of Creation on the seventh day,
and ascended to sit upon his throne of glory. He vested the day of
rest with beauty, and called the Sabbath a delight.

HOPP KOZAK

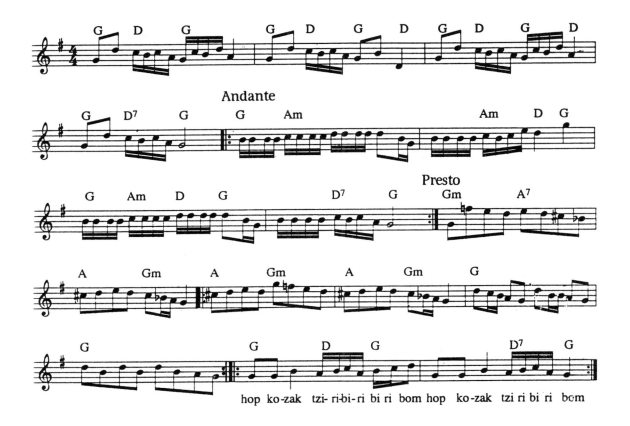

hop ko-zak tzi- ri-bi-ri bi ri bom hop ko-zak tzi ri bi ri bom

The *pritzim* (nobles) ruling the villages in old Russia and Ukraine during the *Shpoler Zayde's* time, used to make sport with their Jewish subjects by dressing them in bearskins and forcing them to dance with a Cossack. When the Jew failed to keep in step with the tune, he would be given lashes with a whip. Once, a Jew who had rented an estate from a noble was imprisoned for failing to pay his rent on time. When he was forced to dance in a bearskin, the *Shpoler Zayde* took the prisoner's place and performed the dance in his stead. Because the *Shpoler Zayde's* dancing was superior, he gained the upper hand over the Cossack. *Hopp Cossack* gives expression to this incident, and for this reason, it opens slowly, gradually working to a climax, aurally depicting the dancer's success and the defeat of his Cossack opponent. It therefore ends with the cry: *Hopp Cossack*. For hasidim of Lubavitch, this song is meant to spur fervent and joyous worship of God. It is sung on *Simchas Toroh* and on other joyous occasions.

NIGUN HAM'SHULOSH

"Besht-Adagio molto religioso

"Magid"-Adagio molto

"Shneur Zalman

The word *Hamshulosh* is derived from the Hebrew *shalosh* (three). Tradition attributes this serious *dvekus* (cleaving) melody to the combined efforts of three great hasidic masters: the Baal Shem Tov (1700-1760), the Magid of Mezeritsch (1710-1772), and the Alter Rebbe, Rabbi Shneur Zalman of Liadi (1747-1813) The three parts are similar. With each succeeding section, however, the *hislahavu*s (flaming ecstasy) increases.

Songs in Yiddish

A DUDELE
CD TRACK No. 8

Rabbi Levi Yitschok of Berditchev

du — du du du du du   miz-roch du ma-riv du — tso-fŏn du — do-rum du

du du du   du du du du du du   du   sho-ma-yim du   o - retz du ———

ma-lo du — ma-to du   du — du du du   du du du du   du du du du

du   du du du du   vu ich ker mich vu ich vend mich   du   du

O Lord of the world, I will sing You a *dudele*. Where can you be found and where can You not be found? Wherever I go and wherever I stand You are there. You, only You, always You. Prosperity is from You, and suffering also comes from You. You are, You were, and You will always be. East, west, north and south are Yours. Heaven and earth are Yours. You take care of the high and the lowly. Wherever I turn, You are there.

This song, in the liturgical-recitative style perfected by Rabbi Levi Yitschok of Berditchev (1740-1810), has become a favorite of singers throughout the world. The text is in Yiddish, and the title of the song is a play on two words: *du* (you,) in this case God, and the primitive shepherd's instrument, the *dudelsack* (bagpipe).

A DIN TOIRE MIT GOTT

Recitativo religioso

Gu_ten mor_gen dir ri_bo_no shel o_lom, ich Lê_vi yitz_chok ben soroh mibar_dit_shev,

ch'bin ge_ku_men tzu dir mit a din tô_roh fun dein folk yis_ro_êl, vos host du tzu dein

folk yis_ro_êl, vos host du zich on_ge_setzt on dein folk yis_ro_êl, az vu nor a_zach iz

e_môr el be_nê yis_ro_êl, az vu nor a_zach iz tzav el be_nê yis_ro_êl, az vu nor a_

zach iz da_bêr el be_nê yis_ro_êl, ta_te_niu zi_ser in himmel, ka_moh u_môs yêsh be_ô_lom?

par_sa_yim, bav_la_yim a_dô_ma_yim. die Russ_lander vos zo_gen? az zei_er Kai_ser iz Kai_ser.
die Deitschlander vos zo_gen? az zei_er mal_chus is mal_chus,

die Englander vos zogen az zei_er mal_chus iz mê_lech, un ich Lê_vi yitz_chok ben so_

roh mi_bar_dit_shev zog: yis_ga_dal ve_yiska_dach shemê ra_boh! un ich Lê_vi yitz_chok ben

so_roh mi_bar_dit_shev zog: lô o_zuz mim_kô_mi, ich vel mich fun ort nicht rih_ren, un a sôf

zol dos nehmen, un an ek zol dos neh_men, yis_ga_dal ve_yis_ka_desh she_mê ra_boh.

"'Good morning, Master of the universe
I, Levi Yitschok of Berditchev
Have come to hold judgment with You
Concerning Your people Israel
What have You against Israel?
Why have you imposed Yourself
Upon Your people Israel?
Everywhere You say:
Command the children of Israel.
Everywhere-Speak to the children of Israel.
Father of mercy
How many nations are there in the world?
Persians, Babylonians, Romans
The Russians— what do they say?
That their emperor is ruler
The Germans—what do they say?
That their Kaiser is King
The English—what do they say?
That their king is ruler
But I Levi-Yitzchok of Berditchev, say
Magnified and sanctified be the Great Name
And I Levi-Yitzchok of Berditchev say:
I will not move from this place, from this very spot
Until there will be an end,
Until there will be an end to this exile
Magnified and sanctified be the Great Name"

MAYERKE MEIN ZUHN

Levi Yitzchok of Berditchev

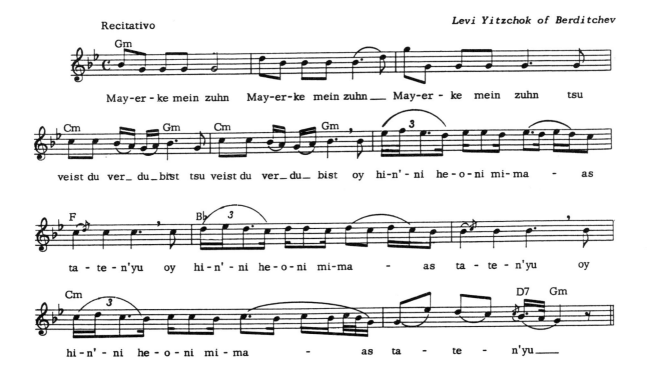

מאיר'קע מיין זון (3)
די ווייסטו ווער דו ביסט (2)
העני העני ממעש סאטעניו (3).

Mayerke, my son, (3)
Do you know who you are? (2)
"Here I stand poor in deeds, dear Father"

This is an example of a hasidic song entering the body of Yiddish folk song. Composed by Rabbi Levi Yitschok of Berditchev, it is set to a Yiddish text, with the opening words of the High Holiday text, *Hin'ni He'oni Mimaas* appearing repeatedly.

HISHTAPCHUS HANEFESH

Menachem Mendl of Vitebsk

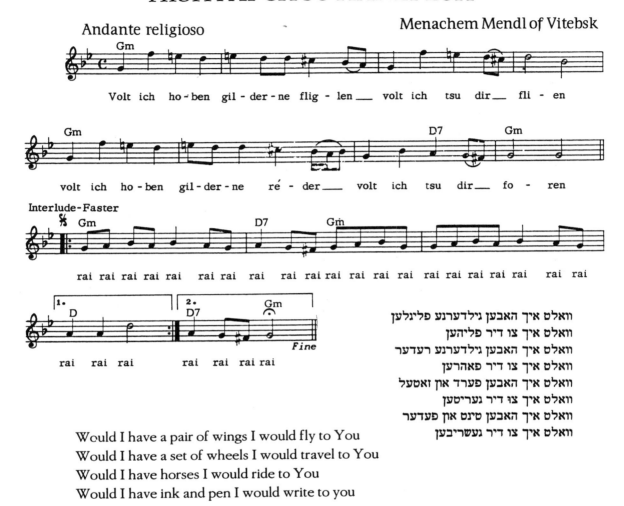

Andante religioso

Volt ich ho-ben gil-der-ne flig-len __ volt ich tsu dir __ fli-en

volt ich ho-ben gil-der-ne ré-der __ volt ich tsu dir __ fo-ren

Interlude-Faster

rai rai rai rai rai rai rai rai rai rai rai rai rai rai rai rai rai rai rai rai rai rai

rai rai rai rai rai rai rai

ווֹאלט איך האבּען גילדערנע פליגלען
ווֹאלט איך צו דיר פליהען
ווֹאלט איך האבּען גילדערנע רעדער
ווֹאלט איך צו דיר פֿאהרען
ווֹאלט איך האבּען פֿערד און זאטעל
ווֹאלט איך צוּ דיר גערײטען
ווֹאלט איך האבּען טינט און פֿעדער
ווֹאלט איך צו דיר געשריבּען

Would I have a pair of wings I would fly to You
Would I have a set of wheels I would travel to You
Would I have horses I would ride to You
Would I have ink and pen I would write to you

Hishtapchus hanefesh (the outpouring of the soul) is in the melodic style of the Ukraine. Attributed to Rabbi Menachem Mendl of Vitebsk (1730-1788), a foremost hasidic figure, the text is completely in Yiddish.

SH'CHINO

Sh'-chi-no Sh'-chi-no vi veit bist du
Go-lus go-lus vi lang bist du
Volt di Sh'-chi-no a-zo veit nit ge-ven
Volt der go-lus nit a-zo lang ge-ven

Sh'chino, Sh'chino how far you are! *Golus, Golus* how large you
are! The *Sh'chino* would not be so far, was the *golus* not so large.

The hasidim of Kalev, Sanz, Bobov, and others set a great number of
texts to this melody. According to tradition, Leib Sarah and his
disdciple Rabbi Isaac of Kalev (according to some variants, it was
Rabbi Hershel of Rimanov) heard a shepherd singing this tune while
tending his flock. The shepherd's song, sung in German, began with
the words *Ros, Ros* (Rose, Rose). Rabbi Isaac of Kalev immediately
changed the words to *Sh'chino, Shchino,* (Divine Presence) and the
new song became a favorite among thousands of hasidim throughout
Europe. When the great hasidic leader, Reb Naftoli of Ropshitz, first
heard it, he proclaimed, "During the time when Rabbi Isaac of Kalev
sang this melody, a great stir was created in the heavens above."

KOL BAYAAR

I hear a voice in the woods. It is the voice of a father calling his
children. A desperate cry of anguish is heard. A father is searching
for his children.

Kol Baya'ar, sung with great feeling by hasidim of Lubavitch, is
noteworthy for its alternate use of Hebrew, Yiddish, and Ukrainian.
It was composed by Reb Aryeh Leib ben Boruch, better known
throughout the hasidic world as the *Shpoler Zayde* (the grandfather
from the Ukrainian city of Shpole). Hasidim relate that the *Shpoler
Zayde* sang *Kol Baya'ar* before the recitation of *Shma Yisroel*
(Hear O Israel) in the evening before retiring, or before *tikun
chatsot* (midnight meditations). In this version, only the Hebrew and
the Yiddish are included.

BRIDER, BRIDER
CD Track No. 11

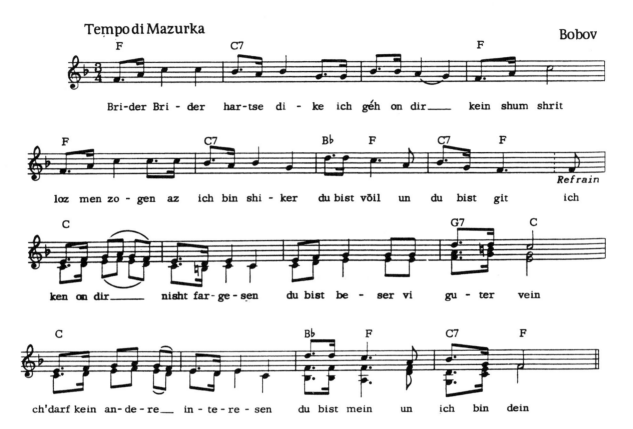

Listen dear brothers! I do not take a single step without you. Let all say that I am drunk. I cannot forget you. You are good, you are wonderful, and you are better than excellent wine. I need no other interests,—I am yours, and you are mine.

At first glance, *Brider, Brider*, appears to be nothing more than a simple love song. It is, however, a love song between man and God. *Brider, Brider*, is jocular in spitrit and is often sung during the Purim festivities by hasidim of Bobov.

ESEN EST ZICH

Lubavitch

E - sen est zich trin - ken trinkt zich vos zol men ton az es

da - vent zich nit e - sen est zich shlo - fen shloft zich vos zol men ton az es

da - vent zich nit_____ e - sen est zich trin - ken trinkt zich vos

zol men ton az es da - vent zich nit_____ e - sen est zich

trin - ken trinkt zich vos zol men ton az es da - vent zich nit

עסען עסט זיך, טרינקען טרינקט זיך
וואס זאל מען טאן. אז עס דאַוונט זיך ניט
עסען עסט זיך, שלאָפען שלאָפט זיך
וואס זאל מען טאן, אז עס דאַוונט זיך ניט.

We eat well, we drink well,
We sleep well
How can we learn to pray well

In this song, the hasid bemoans his failure at not having felt sufficient emotion and inspiration in prayer and the study of Torah. The closing section (coda) expresses the hope of the hasid that he will eventually be able to approach the brilliance and divine radiance of the Lord and his Torah.

NYET NYET NIKAVO

This song is sung with great feeling by Lubavitch Hasidim. The Russian words mean: "There is no one else beside Him." It is a powerful declaration of faith in God, which serves to bolster their commitment to the Torah way of life.

The First "Opera"

The Rebbes of Modzitz are among the few hasidic composers who created sustained, developed works. These large pieces are revered as supreme expressions of devotion in hasidic music; hence they are referred to as "operas" in the sense of masterpieces. Rabbi Saul Taub, the second Rebbe of Modzitz, was the composer of five "operas": this, the first, was written in 1920. It is designed to carry the singers and listeners through various stages of meditation and spiritual awakening until they reach the final ecstasy of joyous communion.

THE FIRST OPERA
CD Track No. 16

GLOSSARY OF FOREIGN TERMS

Adar—Hebrew month.

Capote—Long black coat traditionally worn by hasidim.

Chabad—Lubavitch

Chazan— The appointed and paid precentor of the synagogue.

Dvekus— union, cleaving also a slow rapturous nigun

Eshes Chayil—"A Woman of Valor," recited on Friday evenings

Farbrengen— Hasidic gatherings.

Hakofos— The ritual march of the worshippers carrying the *Toroh* scrolls around the altar on the festival of *Simchas Toroh*

Halacha, Halachic— a generic term for post-Biblical rulings

Hallel—The collective name of Psalms 113 through 118, which are chanted on many festive occasions throughout the year.

Hithlahavus—Flaming ecstacy

Kabbala—Kabbalist mystical teachings of Judaism

Klezmer—lit. instrument of music, a genre of Jewish music

Melave Malke— Meal and Festivities after the end of Sabbath

Midrash—Rabbinic literature, homilies exegesis and sermons based upon the Bible

Misnagdim—Opponents of hasidim.

Mishna — The codification of the oral tradition of basic Jewish law

Mitzva, Mitzvos — Commandment, good deeds

Nigun, Neginah, Nigunim — Melody (ies) especially wordless tunes of the hasidim.

Rebbe — Rabbi or teacher; a hasidic rabbi or leader.

Rikud — Dance.

Rosh Hashonoh — Hebrew "New Year."

Ruach — Spirit

Sephardic — Form of Hebrew pronunciation.

Sh'ma Yisrael — Hear — O Israel. The Jewish profession of faith.

Shabbos — Sabbath

Shacharit year — The morning prayer service

Shovuos — The festival celebrating the gift of the Torah at Mt. Sinai.

Shchino — The Divine Presence — term used in rabbinic literature

Shofar — Ram's horn used in the synagogue during the High Holidays.

Shtibel, Shtiblech — small synagogue or synagogues.

Shul — House of prayer.

Simchas Toroh — Festival which closes the holiday of *Sukot*.

Simcho — Joy, joyous celebration

Talmud — The Oral Law-Body of text comprising the Mishna and commentary and discussions on it

Tikun Chatsos—Midnight Meditations

Tish—Sabbath and Festival meals at the Rebbe's table.

Torah, Toroh—The Bible

Tsadik, Tsadikim— Righteous or saintly being (s).

Yeshiva—Academy of rabbinic and Talmudic learning

Yom Kippur— The "Day of Atonement."

Z'mirot —Domestic Sabbath songs chanted in the home.

Zohar —The title of the fundamental book of the Kabbala